FOAM PATTERNING AND CONSTRUCTION TECHNIQUES

Foam Patterning and Construction Techniques: Turning 2D Designs into 3D Shapes explains how to create your theatrical prop, puppet, or costume design using the unique and tricky medium of foam. Step-by-step instructions, photographs, and explanations illustrate how to translate your design from paper to reality by creating custom "skin" patterns, followed by creation of a foam mock-up. The book details how to bring your project to life with varied finishing techniques, including using fur and fabric coverings and dying and painting foam. Numerous supplies, tools, and safety procedures and protocols are also covered.

- Includes six start-to-finish, step-by-step projects for puppets, masks, and costumes
- Gives practical advice on how to work with foam, including cutting angles, creating curves, and difficult-to-achieve dimensions and shapes
- Provides a thorough review of foam, tools, and safety.

Mary McClung has designed costumes, puppets, masks, and sets for theatre, video, and television for over 17 years. As Artistic Director and craftsperson at Animax Designs, she had the opportunity to design and build for companies such as Disney, Children's Television Workshop, and Universal Studios. McClung has also designed productions with The Dallas Children's Theatre, The Idaho Repertory Theatre, and The Colorado Shakespeare Festival. She teaches full time at West Virginia University as Professor of Costume Design.

FOAM PATTERNING AND CONSTRUCTION TECHNIQUES

TURNING 2D DESIGNS INTO 3D SHAPES

MARY MCCLUNG

Focal Press
Taylor & Francis Group

NEW YORK AND LONDON

First published 2016
by Focal Press
711 Third Avenue, New York, NY 10017

and by Focal Press
2 Park Square, Milton Park, Abingdon, Oxon OX14 4RN

Focal Press is an imprint of the Taylor & Francis Group, an informa business

Library of Congress Cataloging in Publication Data
McClung, Mary, author.
  Foam patterning and construction techniques : turning 2D designs into 3D shapes / Mary McClung.
    pages cm
  Includes bibliographical references and index.
  1. Plastics craft.   2. Plastic foams.   3. Foamed materials.   I. Title.
  TT297.M3764 2016
  745.57'2—dc23   2015030827

ISBN: 978-1-138-01644-6 (hbk)
ISBN: 978-1-138-01643-9 (pbk)
ISBN: 978-1-315-78102-0 (ebk)

Typeset in Univers
by Keystroke, Station Road, Codsall, Wolverhampton

Dedicated to all those creative pups!

contents

Acknowledgments

There is no way I could have finished this book without the support of many good people who were there to discuss ideas, read chapters, and suggest illustration and photo additions.

My very supportive parents, Nanette and Phillip, and my husband Alan are at the top of the list. They never seemed to tire of my "nannering" about edits and questions concerning what would help to better explain an idea or technique.

Special thanks to the West Virginia University faculty, staff, and students who took on extra work to support my sabbatical, allowing me to flesh out and finish the writing and illustrations.

Thank you to Kim at *Fabric on a Roll* for allowing me to wander around her store, snapping photos.

Special thanks to Henry, Penny, Scottie, Annie, Zoe, Ripley, Scout, and Alan for patiently posing for photos illustrating fur direction and armor.

Preface

The goal of this book is to introduce the reader to the different ways of developing patterns for foam fabrication. There are many different kinds of foams and though there is a brief mention of rigid foams in Chapter 1, the focus is primarily in the area of those foams that are flexible. In the process of writing I decided to expand into the areas of design and finishing techniques to show a little of the preparation and follow-through that is needed to help facilitate the process. Hopefully, with the addition of the characters "Scout" and "the Professor", all of this will help flesh-out and provide a bit more depth to a somewhat dry subject.

Sadly, organic chemistry is not my area so please forgive the very generic explanations of how foams were invented and are made. It is a fascinating subject but not, I thought, crucial to this book. If one were interested in pursuing a bit more information about the history of foam, there are dozens of websites and publications dedicated to this subject.

The book is laid out by sections starting with tools, safety, and choosing the right foam for the project. Sections II through VI take the reader through different parts of the process of foam construction: design, differing patterning techniques, how to translate the design into 3D, how to divide patterns, how to cut foam to get the desired shape, and, finally, the different ways to finish foam objects. The final section takes the reader through five specific projects utilizing all the techniques explained throughout the book.

As far as working with the medium of foam is concerned, those who work with it have their favorite tools and ways of working that may or may not be covered in this book. I am sure too that there are many old and new products not mentioned here that have tried and true uses. The majority of the patterning techniques that are reviewed in this book are based on the "draping" process associated with costume pattern making. These techniques involve starting with a foundation shape and then creating a skin from which the pattern is derived. Any artisan or craftsperson who works with foam has their own variation on these same techniques and there is no one process that is necessarily the right way, but hopefully this book will provide a foundation on which to start and grow.

Above all else take these suggestions, be safe, be patient, and have great fun making wonderful things.

Thank you.
Mary McClung

SECTION I

THE MEDIUM OF FOAM: MATERIALS, TOOLS, AND SAFETY

chapter one

materials: foams, tools for shaping, cutting surfaces, and adhesives

This chapter provides an overview of foams and some of the items used for shaping and patterning.

Foam

There are many different varieties of foams. Whether it is for structure, flexibility, or mold ability, each foam is produced and developed for a specific use. With a little artistic planning and experimentation, foam has been and can continue to be adapted and used for many nontraditional projects that utilize the same properties.

The discovery and/or development of the basic ingredients (isocyanates, polymeric polyols, styrols, isobutylene, etc.) for the manufacturing of almost all plastics and foams are a result of the petrochemical and coal industries. There are a few exceptions to this wherein a discovery of a substance or chemical was made as a result of experimentation with living plants or animals. For the most part these early endeavors were expanded upon and modified using contemporary technology. Now there are an abundance of foams used for everything from packaging and soundproofing, to floatation and food handling.

Many of these foams do not degrade quickly and can last for hundreds of years in landfills. Foams and their additives are also becoming more integrated into our soil and water. Fortunately there have been successful efforts in reducing the toxicity levels of foam additives; lowering VOC (volatile organic compound) levels and creating foams that are biodegradable made from vegetable oils and starches such as soy and corn.

How Foam is Made

The most basic explanation of how foam is produced is that liquid *base A* and liquid *foaming agent B* are combined. While the foaming agent reacts and produces air pockets expanding the

The Creation of Foam.

possible to have custom thicknesses cut for the needs of the project.

Types of Flexible Foam

mass of the mixture, this produces heat, called an *exothermic reaction*. When the mixture has reached its maximum expansion, it cures becoming soft or rigid, and foam is produced. Chemical variations in the base and the foaming agent will produce a variety of textures, pore sizes, flexibilities, and densities. When beginning to build up a knowledge of different foams, it is important to be able to touch and handle all the varieties available. When ordering online, try to get samples to familiarize yourself with various products. This will help you to know what type of foam might be best for any future applications.

When prefabricated at foam manufacturers, liquid batches of some types of foams are mixed in large vats and poured into molds. When the foam is fully expanded and cured in block form, it is called a *bun*. The bun is cut to the desired widths (planks, profiles, sheets) by using tools such as a large horizontal band saw, a precision laser, or a cutting machine using a water jet. Depending on the type of flexible foam and where you buy it, commercial thicknesses can range from 1/4 inch and up. Rigid foams such as expanded polystyrene foams can be purchased in huge blocks and slabs. If you go to a manufacturer where foam is made, it is sometimes also

• **Closed-cell foam**—*Closed-cell, mini-cell, cross-linked polyethylene, fun foam, L 200*: all of these are names for lightweight foam that is great for carving, sanding, and constructing. It is very dense, allows for little to no water absorption, but is soft. The flexibility can vary depending on the thickness and density. This foam paints really well with a brush or an airbrush. Thin widths of closed-cell foam (1/8 inch to 1/4 inch) can be shaped using a hot hair dryer without scorching or melting. L 400 and L 600 are denser varieties of this foam—the greater the number the more dense and structural the foam. The 1/2-inch thick, gray, anti-fatigue mats are a popular and very accessible type of mini-cell foam which can be purchased at stores such as Harbor Freight and Lowes.

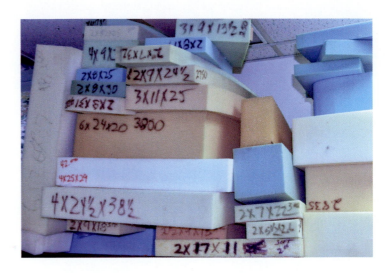

Figure 1-2: Polyether foam, also called upholstery foam, comes in a variety of colors and widths. The color variations can represent different densities (firmness) and longevity.

Figure 1-1:

A. Closed-cell foam also called L 200, mini-cell, and generically, cross-linked polyethylene foam (depending on the manufacturer).

B. Mini-cell foam can be purchased in 1/8-inch sheets, called fun foam, in many colors and textures.

- **Open-cell foam**—Developed in the 1940s, liquid urethane was first used for coatings on airplanes. It was discovered that the addition of polyols would expand and form a porous material. These first foams were used for floatation and insulation. Urethane foams are now used for everything from filtration and soundproofing to packaging, large-scale industrial fabrication, and special effects.

- **Polyether urethane foam**—When inquiring about *polyether* foam it might be referred to as: *urethane ether foam, urethane foam, craft foam,* or *upholstery foam.* This foam is very soft, has small pores, and is flexible. It can be carved, sanded (using a belt sander), glued, patterned into shapes, dyed (test to make certain), and airbrushed. Due to its chemical composition it is somewhat fragile and is not suited for hand sewing without reinforcement or for machine sewing. It is also not as durable as *polyester* (reticulated foams). It will eventually disintegrate when exposed to sunlight and moisture; however, if covered with fabric (as with furniture upholstery or covering a foam puppet), it may last for many years depending on the amount of use. It is readily available and can be found in local craft and fabric stores as well as those businesses specializing in upholstery.

Figure 1-3: Notice the small pore size of polyether foam.

Though prices have risen considerably, polyether urethane foam is cheaper than most other foams and easier to find. Polyether foam is my first choice for building mock-ups of newly patterned shapes. There are many different grades varying from a slightly crisper, low cost, less durable foam to a softer, denser, and more durable variety found in green, blue, and white.

- **Polyester urethane foam**—Also known as reticulated foam, scot foam, or filtration foam, polyester urethane foam is very durable, flexible, paintable, dye-able and, depending on the height of the machine presser foot, it can be sewn on a machine or by hand (if using a commercial machine, 1/4 to 1 inch is the maximum

Figure 1-4: Tiger head in mini-cell foam and a mock-up in less expensive upholstery foam.

Figure 1-5: Sample widths of reticulated foam. When urethane foams are fresh they are cream-colored but they yellow with age.

suggested width). It comes in white or black. The *ppi* (pores per square inch) can vary affecting the surface look of the piece. Though every foam crafter has their favorite, I find that a polyester or reticulated foam ranging from 30 to 35 ppi works well.

- **Expandable polyurethane cold foam**—This form of urethane foam may be called *cold foam, expandable cold foam,* or *polyurethane cold foam.* It is the same material as the prefabricated urethane panels and buns as previously mentioned. Even though it does produce heat during the exothermic reaction before curing, it is called cold foam because unlike *foam latex* (sometimes called hot foam because it needs to be baked to cure) it does not require a low heat oven to go through its final curing process. What sets this form of urethane foam apart is that it comes in a two-part, liquid kit that can be mixed by the individual crafter and poured into custom molds for masks, rigid prosthetics, props, etc. The kits can be for rigid or soft consistencies. Depending on the manufacturer, foam weights can range anywhere from around three to nine pounds. When dealing

A.

B.

C.

Figure 1-6: Both rigid and flexible foams look the same. The chemical formula determines the final flexibility or rigidity.
A. Cross-section of cold foam.
B. Nose prosthetic and mask made with flexible cold foam.
C. Rigid cold foam.

with *soft* cold foam kits, the lower numerical number indicates a lower density and therefore a more flexible foam. The *rigid* cold foam kits are listed similarly with the lower numerical number indicating weight and a lower density; they are therefore lighter, more porous, and easier to carve and shape.

This is also the foam that is sprayed into house walls, and around doors and windows for insulation. It can be purchased premixed with propellant in small cans, or is installed by insulation companies in large, premixed batches blown into house walls with hoses. It starts out as a liquid then expands into nooks and crannies, hardening and sealing as it cures.

- **Polyethylene foam**—*Polyethylene foam* or *ethyfoam* is a semi-soft to firm foam that can be carved, sanded, cut, etc.

Figure 1-7: Polyethylene foam comes in a variety of widths, profiles, and colors. Shown is gray ethyfoam rod used for insulation and white custom packing material.

It is commonly used for insulation, floatation, and for packaging to dampen vibration. It is fairly dense, yet resilient, and when sanded the surface can become a bit fibrous until sealed or covered. When ordering polyethylene foam be careful to not confuse it with *cross-linked* polyethylene foam or you might be receiving mini-cell foam by mistake.

Types of Rigid Foam

There are many varieties of rigid foams available for the foam artisan. The following are a few types.

- **Polystyrene foam: expanded and extruded**—When rigid foams are mentioned often the most common foam that comes to mind is polystyrene or by its trade name *Styrofoam*. The main ingredient of polystyrene plastic, *styrol,* was discovered in the mid-1800s as a resin derived from a Turkish gum tree.

In the late 1930s, the Dow Chemical Company experimented by adding isobutylene to a form of styrol and the material *Styrofoam* was created. Its earliest uses were for floatation but it was soon recognized for its high insulating

Figure 1-8: Expanded polystyrene foam or bead board.

Figure 1-9: Extruded polystyrene foam board.

characteristics. In addition to those tried and true uses, it is now used as lightweight substructures for floors and walls, and the uses keep coming.

Expanded polystyrene, *EPS*, or *bead board* is one form of polystyrene foam. It can be found in extruded sheets, giant blocks, molded shapes, and in bags of individual beads. It commonly appears on store shelves as extruded shapes such as coolers and food containers. Other uses include props as well as extremely large scenic pieces used in television, theater, and motion pictures.

Extruded polystyrene board, extruded polystyrene, or *foam board* is the second, denser form of polystyrene foam

used primarily for insulation. It comes in four foot by eight foot sheets in various thicknesses. Colors include green, pink, and blue.

Both of these forms of polystyrene foam are very lightweight, relatively inexpensive, and can be carved, painted, and sanded with relative ease.

- **Rigid urethane foam**—Commonly used in the marine and aeronautics industries, this foam can vary from being semi-hard (low density) to rock hard (high density). Depending on the density, it can be sanded, shaped on a lathe, drilled, cut, and carved. It can be purchased in boards and in blocks pre-cured from art supply, hobby, automotive, and marine supply stores.

As mentioned previously, there are also two-part kits for rigid foam that can be mixed to allow for pouring into custom molds.

Figure 1-10: Both low and high-density rigid foams can look the same but they feel very different.

A. A variety of samples of low and high-density foam provided by General Plastics.

B. Low-density balsa foam.

C. Rigid high-density foam insulation.

Cutting and Shaping Tools

There are many options when cutting and shaping flexible and rigid foam. Below are a few commonly used tools.

Cutting Foam!

- **Single-edged razor blades**—Sizes can range from 1 1/2 inches to 2 inches. These have been commonly used for shaving and paint scraping. When used with foam, razor blades are invaluable for cutting precise, clean angles. These blades are very sharp but will dull quickly when cutting foam. It's a good idea to purchase a blade sharpener to use while you are working.

Tip

Used razor blades should be placed in a container such as an empty soda can, before throwing away because they will cut through garbage bags. The blades are usually steel and can be recycled. Call your local recycling company to find out how the blades should be packaged for handling. Some recycling companies will not take them because blades can get caught in machinery or are a danger to employees.

- **Box cutter, utility knife, or carpet knife**—This tool consists of a hollow handle that houses a steel cutting blade. Some of these are retractable for safety. The handle is easily unscrewed for storing extra blades. The blades by themselves can be useful as they are 2 inches or more in length and can help when cutting foam that is thick.
- **X-acto knife**—An x-acto knife comprises a handle which when twisted will clamp onto the steel blade. These knives are also very sharp and will last a little longer than razor blades. There are many varieties and sizes of blades. Though these are precision tools, I have found that they give you less dexterity and fluidity when cutting foam compared to razor blades.
- **Scissors**—Scissors are a quick way of cutting foam. There are different grades of scissors—often the higher the cost the better the quality. These are great for cutting thinner foam (no thicker than 1/2 inch). Thicker foam cut with scissors can result in loss of precision and choppy, rough edges.
- **Band saw**—The band saw is an upright electric saw with a narrow *band* blade (starting at 1/8 inch and up) that circulates on internal wheels. It is especially good when cutting blocks of soft urethane, and mini-cell foam. Care should be taken to let the blade do the work and not to push the foam with too much force. Goggles and a dust mask are recommended when using this tool.
- **Electric knife**—This is a knife that is traditionally used for carving meat. It can be used with soft upholstery, and reticulated foams as well as closed-cell foams.
- **Hot wire tool**—Used for carving polystyrene foam, the hot wire tool consists of a wire pulled taut between metal arms. It is an electric tool through which current is generated that heats the wire. When the wire is pressed against the foam it melts and therefore cuts its way through the foam. This tool can be table-sized to cut giant blocks of foam or a small hand-held variety for sculpting small details. Gases released during the melting of the polystyrene foam are toxic. A respirator gauged to filter the specific fumes emanating

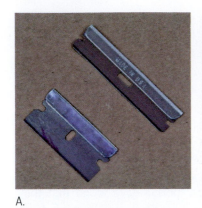

A.

B.

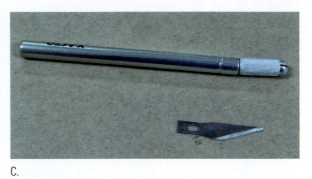

C.

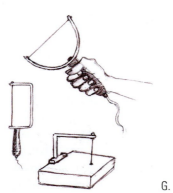

D.

E.

F.

G.

H.

I.

J.

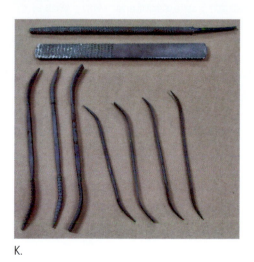

K.

L.

Figure 1-11:

A. Single-edged razor blades.
B. Examples of utility knives: carpet knife and
   extendable cutter with disposable tips.
C. X-acto knife.
D. Scissors.
E. Band saw.
F. Electric knife.

G. Hot wire tool.
H. Belt sander.
I. Dremel tool.
J. Shurform tools.
K. Rasps and files.
L. Sandpaper.

Figure 1-12: When foam is too thick to cut with scissors a rough edge will result.

during the burning/melting process is recommended. See *Chapter 2*.

- **Belt sander**—Belt sanders come in different varieties ranging from small for detailed pieces to large for sanding big areas. These electric tools are commonly used for sanding wood. However after the basic silhouette or form is cut, the belt sander can be used to shape soft or rigid urethane and closed-cell foams.
- **Dremel tool**—The dremel tool is an invaluable, hand-held (electric or battery-operated) tool for working on many projects. It is useful for sanding and cutting hard to reach nooks and crannies and for large carved or sculpted areas on objects made out of soft or rigid urethane or closed-cell foams. There are many different *bits* and attachments that can be purchased separately as needed. Make sure to test the various bits on a scrap piece of foam before jumping into the real thing. A dust mask and goggles are recommended when using this tool.
- **Shurform tools, rasps, and files**—The best hand-held tools for shaping and smoothing foam are shurform tools, rasps, and files. These come in a variety of shapes from rods and slightly convex to pointy, tooth-like shapes with abrasive surfaces for small, tight areas. These tools are used for semi-rigid (such as ethyfoam) and rigid foams.
- **Sandpaper**—Sandpaper is another great tool to assist with refining surfaces on rigid foams. The number on the back of each paper determines sandpaper abrasiveness; the lower the number the larger the grit of the sandpaper and the more coarse and rough the surface. Sandpaper that is 60–80 grit is very coarse and is great for sanding surfaces that are rough and highly textured. The finer grits of 150 and higher can be used to further sand surfaces to an even smoother texture. Some sandpaper works well with a little moisture, this is called *wet sanding*. The moisture acts as a lubricant to help with any friction that might occur by moving the loose grit and particulate around on the surface. The finest sanding is called *buffing* and it is done on surfaces such as stone, metal, and some plastics and resins to encourage a high sheen or clarity. A fibrous cloth or pad is often used when this level of polishing is needed. The dremel tool has both sanding and buffing attachments.

Cutting and Work Surfaces

Foam Cutting Back!

The best surfaces on which to cut are those that are smooth and present little drag or friction. This improves the dexterity of your hand as it cuts and helps to preserve the cutting edge of the blade for as long as possible.

Figure 1-14: Homasote made from cellulose fiber.

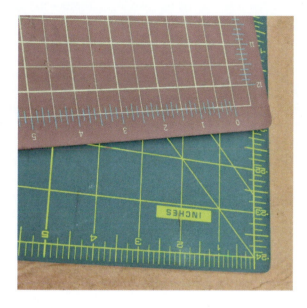

Figure 1-13: Cutting mats can range in size and color.

- **Cutting mats**—Commonly used by quilters and stencil artists, these are commonly found in gray or green colors, and are printed with a grid. They also come in various sizes. I would suggest purchasing the biggest you can afford, as they are very useful for preserving the worktable surface as well as floor treatments. I say this after having damaged wooden tabletops and floors, carpeting, linoleum, etc. There is a slight drag associated with these mats and they will show some wear after repeated use. However these are really tough and are the most reliable surface for repeated cutting with metal blades.
- **Homasote**—This material can be found at most home improvement stores in four foot by eight foot sheets, is 1/2 inch thick, and can easily be cut down to custom sizes using a jig saw (with a sturdy blade), table saw, or circular hand saw. It is made from compressed cellulose fiber and is used for soundproofing and bulletin boards. Homasote is an excellent surface foundation for tables when cutting fabric or foam and for paper pattern layout. It makes a sturdy and smooth surface for pushpins. It is very durable, but will eventually develop cutting wear and tear. Homasote needs to be covered if liquid is being used as the cellulose fiber could absorb moisture and warp the surface. To help preserve the surface from daily wear, it's advisable to cover it with paper, fabric, or a waterproof material.
- **Cork**—Homasote has replaced cork for most worktable and bulletin board surfaces, but cork is an outstanding table surface. The best cork is that which is the least pitted and, when covered with paper as a protective surface, it can last a long time. Cork is a renewable product taken from peeling the secondary surface layer from the living cork oak tree. These trees can live to be 300 years old and can be used for harvesting cork repeatedly without killing the tree.

Figure 1-15: Cork tabletop.

Adhesives

Ready to Glue!

Adhesives for Flexible Foam

When gauging what is the best adhesive to use, generally it is the one that simulates or preserves the inherent qualities of the foundation material. Wood workers use poly vinyl acetate glues that dry hard, bonding two rigid materials together. However if a rigid adhesive such as wood glue (PVA (poly vinyl acetate)) is applied to flexible foam, the glue joint could break or tear the foam because the joint does not flex with the rest of the material. The appropriate adhesives to use with flexible foam are those that maintain the flexibility. These are called *contact adhesives* and are commonly used to glue leather, rubber, fabrics, linoleum, carpeting, veneer, and, most importantly, flexible foam. A contact adhesive works on a molecular level because it consists of hundreds of polymer chains which when touched get tangled together and interconnect. Therefore when using contact adhesives the process involves coating *both surfaces* to be attached, and letting the adhesive dry (dry meaning losing most of its solvent or carrier). The two surfaces are then pressed firmly together; thus the name *contact adhesive*. When contact adhesives are used appropriately, the two sides coated with glue will adhere with only a slight pressure. It is not necessary to clamp the pieces together. There is however a working time and if left for too long the glue will dry completely or "set up" and lose its ability to adhere.

Some types of these adhesives will allow for a "pulling apart and repositioning period", but generally you get one chance to put them together accurately. If the sides are pulled apart too many times, no matter which adhesive is being used, it will lose its ability to stick and more will need to be applied.

Some uses for contact cement include gluing rubber soles to shoes and also attaching layers of leather together. In these situations after the initial contact between the two pliable surfaces has been made, it is a good idea to pound the two pieces together using a broad-headed hammer or mallet. This step removes trapped air and will press any unseen, non-bonded areas firmly together.

In the past contact adhesives were known for possessing highly toxic fumes that were harmful when inhaled, possibly affecting the central nervous system, internal organs, and respiratory system. Fortunately they now come in two types: *low VOC* and *high VOC*. VOC stands for *volatile organic compounds* meaning the harmful gases released when certain products are used.

Tip

One way to tell when contact adhesives are ready to bond is by touching the surface. Contact adhesive should not come off on your fingers. If it does this means the solvent supplied to move the polymer chains around has not had a chance to evaporate and expose the chains. Allow more time for the adhesive to dry but not too much or the "adhesion window" will be lost.

- **Low VOC contact adhesives**—These products are sold commercially and use neoprene or liquid rubber as a main ingredient for adhesion. See *Chapter 2*.

These adhesives are very useful when working on foam projects indoors and are a welcome change. They are relatively easy to use but can add additional time to the fabrication process. The amount of adhesive used and the surface of the foam can affect the working time, i.e. the more porous the foam the longer it can take to get a good bond. In terms of application, when working with neoprene or rubber-based adhesives very little is needed to achieve a bond; *less is more* and it should be applied as evenly as possible. Using a hand-held hair dryer helps to speed up the drying time. It is best to experiment with these and all new materials before jumping into the actual project. These adhesives need careful monitoring as they can "set up" and lose their ability to adhere unpredictably.

Table 1.1: Adhesives

Adhesive	Type	Use	Dry time	Adhering ability	VOC
Locktite Foamboard Adhesive	neoprene-based contact cement	adhere soft foams, fabric, etc.	fast with hair dryer	excellent	very low
Weldwood Green Contact Adhesive	neoprene-based contact cement	adhere soft foams, fabric, etc.	moderately fast with hair dryer	difficult to work with	very low
Simalfa	neoprene-based contact cement	adhere soft foams	fast with hair dryer	good	very low
Barge Glue/Cement	tolulene-based contact adhesive	soft foams, leather, rubber	fast	excellent	very high
Weldwook (red can) Contact Adhesive	tolulene-based contact adhesive	soft foams, leather, rubber	fast	excellent	very high
Liquid Nails	paste-like adhesive	glue rigid foams	long drying	strong	low
Elmer's and Titebond Wood Glue	PVA glues	rigid foam	medium	excellent	low
3M Super 77	spray adhesive	rigid and flexible foams	fast	good	very high
Fast Bond Contact Adhesive	contact adhesive	rigid foam	fast to medium	N/A	N/A
Great Stuff Pro Adhesive	expandable foam adhesive	rigid foam	fast	excellent—but will push the foam apart	very high

Figure 1-16: A variety of low VOC contact adhesives for flexible foam.

taped closed), because the shelf life of an opened container is six months.

Note: there is always the chance that anybody could have a bad reaction to a product. Even though a product says "low" or "no" VOC, use with caution.

Titebond also produces two different contact adhesives in smaller cans that are outstanding adhesives for foam. See *Table 1.1* for a list of adhesives and their characteristics.

• **High VOC contact adhesives**—These are powerful adhesives. In addition to durability, they also dry quickly (even quicker with a hair dryer) and are not as finicky as the neoprene-based and rubber-based adhesives in terms of how much you apply. However, even with these adhesives, a neat, even coat will always be better than a giant, uncontrollable glob. The major drawback to these conventional contact cements is the toxicity levels you

The exceptions to the above description are the adhesives produced by the Simalfa Company. Their claim is that only one side of the two pieces needs to be coated with adhesive and it is ready to bond together on contact. The application they recommend is by spraying a fine mist. Without the equipment to spray the product, you need to dab on a very sheer film on both sides of the foam. The proper amount can be achieved with practice. It does dry very fast (I still recommend a hair dryer), is strong, and dries clear. They kindly sent me a sample of one of their products (Simalfa 309). I have colleagues who have used their products and swear by them. The smallest amount sold is five gallons so it is a good idea to decant it into smaller, sealable bottles (recycled juice bottles with the lids

Figure 1-17: A variety of high VOC contact adhesives.

are exposed to when using them. If you choose to use them, work outside with a slight breeze and wear a respirator gauged to filter the specific gases associated with the adhesive you are using. For more information see *Chapter 2*.

Adhesives for Rigid Foam

Figure 1-18: Paste-like foam adhesives.

Because the industrial uses of rigid foams generally supersede the artistic, a lot of the adhesives you find are gauged to adhere rigid foam to masonry walls (cement or stone) or wood. Adhesives such as *Loctite Foamboard Adhesive* and *Liquid Nails* have been formulated to be thick and paste-like to allow for better surface area adhesion to porous surfaces. Though not meant for this purpose, these can be used to glue several layers of foam together to create a larger foam block for carving and shaping but can create a dense seam line when attempting to sand smooth the surface, which adds more time to the sculpting process. This adhesive may take several days to dry when clamped between pieces of foam.

Figure 1-19: Contact adhesive marketed for rigid foam.

There are thinner adhesives such as 3M's *Super 77 Spray Adhesive* and *Fast Bond Contact Adhesive* (thinly brushed, rolled, or sponged on). When used with foams that produce lots of dry particles, these adhesives can pull apart unexpectedly if any foam dust has interfered with the adhesion process. If care is taken to prepare the surface to be glued, these adhesives generally have very good adhesion. They will dry within a couple of hours.

Another adhesive is the Dow Company's *Great Stuff Pro Adhesive* (http://greatstuff.dow.com/products/pro/wall-and-floor). This is expandable urethane foam in a can. When cold foam is in its liquid form it is extremely sticky or, as the company states, "provides a fast-grab tack". The drawback is that it may push apart the foam pieces and can add additional thickness to the foam being glued. Clamping between pieces of wood or adding applied weight is recommended to help alleviate some of the expansion and to help keep the foam from cracking because of the pressure of expansion. This adhesive will cure in approximately 30 minutes.

Figure 1-20: Examples of poly vinyl acetate adhesives commonly used for carpentry, but are also handy for rigid foam.

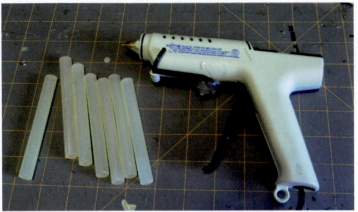

Figure 1-21: Hot glue gun and sticks.

Hot Glue

Hot glue is a very popular method of joining materials together. The "glue" is heated/melted plastic and with additional layers can cover or encase whatever it is being applied to. Hot glue comes in low and high temperature varieties and the method of dispensing can range from a dipping pot, mini glue guns, and standard sized guns to a gun with a fine, pencil-tip point. Hot glue is not commonly used for joining foam parts together. Even though the glue when cooled is somewhat flexible it can form a clunky seam between foam pieces, can restrict flexibility, and add weight. When applied it can also melt or retract some rigid foams compromising the joining of pieces by reducing the surface area. However, despite the drawbacks, some foam artisans swear by hot glue. I find it is especially handy for finishing techniques such as gluing feathers, teeth, and other extraneous parts.

Tip
Always test adhesives and paints when starting a project. Some products might have quirky drying times or could even dissolve your foam.

PVA glues or wood glues produced by companies such as Titebond and Elmers are also good to use with rigid foam, but can take a few days to dry. Clamping or compressing with weight is recommended to help support the bond. The dried seams will be tight and sharp and will need a little extra attention when sanding.

A.

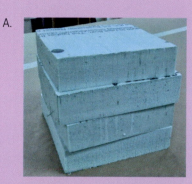

B.

Figure 1-22:
A. Stack of glued extruded blue polystyrene foam.
B. Glued stack of various polystyrene foams.

When using many layers of rigid foam glued together, it is recommended to try and use the same type of foam. For example, if using expanded polystyrene use a stack of this foam throughout, or if using extruded foam board try to stay with this same type.

These foams have different densities and strengths and, when sculpting, softer foam will sand away faster than more rigid foam. Bead foam is not only a different texture but it is also softer than extruded foam and the two glued together to create a sculpted object would cause an irregular sanding surface adding time to the process. In the end, however, it is not impossible to achieve a good-looking

piece with a mixture of foams but it can complicate the process.

Figure 1.23: Carved and painted polystyrene puppet.

chapter two

safety

The purpose of this chapter is to give a brief overview of safety awareness. There is so much information available to the public about safe practices that many entire books have been dedicated to this subject and rightly so. There are many ways we can damage others and ourselves without intending to. It is surprising, scary, and truly fascinating what is taken for granted as being "safe".

Perhaps defining the term "safe" is a good place to start. The term "safe" when discussing effects of toxins and using tools could perhaps be defined as "causing no physical harm or damage". This begs the question: is it possible to live and function in our world without some harm being done to us physically? The answer could be "yes" if we lived in a bubble. However, if the answer is "no", then perhaps a better definition of "safe" is " *minimizing* the risk of physical harm or damage". In terms of the self-preservation instinct, no one wants "physical harm or damage" imposed on him or her, but the reality is that as we live our lives logically there will be some effects imposed on us by just existing in this world. The food we eat, the water we drink, the cleaning supplies we use, the clothes we wear, our building materials, the sunlight, the air, using tobacco, the medicines we use, the list goes on and on. The point being that it is impossible to eliminate all the potentially bad things we are exposed to, but we can have some control over selecting what we work with and how we use it. *Yes* there will be some exposure to harmful vapors and materials, *yes* there will be risk involved, but we owe it to ourselves and others to proceed with knowledge and care.

The hope is that this chapter will shed a little light on potentially dangerous processes, how chemicals and working with tools can sometimes be bad for us, and (most important of all), how we can make working with foam as safe as possible. Let's face it: if you choose to work with foam, many of the materials associated with foam construction can be harmful. The question is: don't we want to be healthy for as long as we can so we will be able to design and build wonderful things for as long as possible? I say "Yes, yes, yes!"

Chemical Awareness

Many products are harmful if used incorrectly and without the proper safety gear. With the exception of perhaps the cutting surfaces, all the tools and materials listed in *Chapter 1* can be dangerous. Toxins are perhaps the most insidious because these often go unnoticed and can enter the human body through skin, eyes, mouth, and nose. However, equally as dangerous are mishandling tools and not wearing standard safety gear. The good news is that most of the hazards can be minimized and even avoided with a little research and applied common sense. This chapter will provide some basic information for guidance.

Material Safety Data Sheets, Safety Data Sheets, and the Global Harmonized System

From cleaning supplies to adhesives, to cornstarch and axle grease—you can find an MSDS and a SDS on almost anything. These can be found by searching the Web, and sometimes will be included in the packaging of mail-ordered products. The *Material Safety Data Sheet* (MSDS) and the *Safety Data Sheet* (SDS) are documents available to the public that generally list: the contents/chemicals in a given product, any hazards that could occur when using the product, toxicology tests and their results, suggested first aid treatments, and how to clean up safely. The *Occupational Safety and Health Administration* (OSHA) is in the process of changing the MSDS to the Global Harmonized System (GHS) for its hazard communication standard. The MSDS was already very informative but this new system is designed to clearly standardize each category listed and is now called simply Safety Data Sheet (SDS). Information about the new communication standards and the SDS can be found at the OSHA's website: https://www.osha.gov/dsg/hazcom/index.html.

Safety Gear

Along with information about what specific chemicals or ingredients you are being exposed to, the MSDS and SDS can be handy tools for determining what safety equipment will be needed. For example, when buying a respirator, the safety supplier's website or customer service department will often be able to tell you what sort of filter cartridges are needed for the respirator by inquiring about the type of chemicals you will be using. Respirator cartridges are designed for specific chemicals. The MSDS and SDS list by percentage the chemicals included in the product, thus you will be able to purchase the correct respirator filter to use the product safely.

The same is true for hand protection. There are many different kinds of gloves available for working with different chemicals. Never assume that a latex or vinyl glove is what should be used because that is what is available at your local Wal-Mart. Some gloves will react with chemicals and dissolve, and some could even react with a chemical, damage your skin, and pass into your body. The advice here is to take a few minutes to research the products you are using and the appropriate *Personal Protective Equipment* (PPE) needed to be safe.

Ideal Ventilation

What does "a well-ventilated area" mean? This phrase is often included with the directions on many products that are volatile or toxic, pertaining to vapors or dust that are combustible, can contaminate breathable air space, or be absorbed through the skin. The best ventilation situation in which to use these sorts of products is outside, if there is a light breeze, even better. *Note*: even though you may be outside, it is still advisable to wear the appropriate safety gear.

Unfortunately many products do not work well in high humidity, when it is raining, or when the temperature falls below 50 degrees Fahrenheit. Therefore, when used indoors, the well-ventilated area means a cross ventilation set-up. For example, two open windows wherein the air comes in one window (propelled by a fan) and sweeps the fumes outside through the other window. Other examples include: an open garage door with a breeze (because you are basically removing a whole wall), and working in front of a fan that blows the fumes outside. *Note*: even with these examples the proper safety gear should be worn.

When using a fan remember merely circulating air within an enclosed space does not mean "well ventilated". The

Figure 2-1: Suggested layout of well-ventilated area.

vapors need an exit route and a fresh air source to push them out and away from you.

Ventilated chemical or *spray booths* are another option and are wonderful if you can afford to install them. Generally mounted in a metal shell, an exhaust fan draws the dust and vapors away from the working area, larger particulates are collected in a filter, and the vapors are sucked outside. If you are lucky enough to have a spray booth this will streamline your fabrication process. Hopefully the outside exhaust from the booth has not been placed near the *air intake* for the building in which you are working!

A great piece of advice is: *be aware of your work area.* Again common sense, but when you get excited about a project it is hard to step back and take the time to set up a safe work environment not only for yourself but those working beside you.

Figure 2-2: A respirator and a dust mask.

Tip

Things to consider when using volatile chemicals or when producing flammable dust:

- There could be open flames like pilot lights nearby, which could react to any combustible material such as sawdust or gaseous fumes that are in the air.
- Be aware of where the air intake to your building is positioned. If you see people doing something questionable such as smoking or spray painting by this area you may want to encourage them to move away.
- If you wear a respirator and are sharing a workspace with others, then they need to wear a respirator too.

Dust Mask Vs. Respirator: Which to Use?

When it comes to a dust mask or a respirator, one of the best ways to decide which to wear is whether you can smell the product. If the product has a smell then a respirator should be worn. There are some products, however, that produce odorless vapors or gases that can be dangerous when inhaled (for example some expandable cold foams). Again read the product packaging and the OSHA safety sheets. Make sure you wear the recommended PPE needed to make the project not be your last.

The best news is that many companies are now producing safer products that contain low or non-toxic compounds. For example, BJB is now selling low di-isocyanate cold foam. This does not mean that the product is completely non-toxic but rather that one or more of the especially harmful toxins and gases have been reduced. However, it is a great step in the right direction. Let us hope more companies do the same!

Always check the company's website and the MSDS or SDS of the products you are considering. Companies will also often have technical advisors on the staff to answer any questions you might have. Take the time to explain your projects and develop relationships with these folks. They may be able to recommend other products you have not considered.

Dust masks (and respirators) are used in situations where there is large and small dust particulate in the air. Use a dust

Tip

Respirator tests are recommended for respirators that are used regularly. These tests gauge to see if the respirator is the proper size and shape to fit the face. If there are gaps between the face and the respirator, harmful vapors can be drawn in with inhalation thus bypassing the filters and rendering the respirator useless.

Tip

Respirator cartridges have a limited life span. When exposed to certain chemicals, cartridges may only be able to effectively filter for a certain amount of time and will need to be replaced. When not using the respirator, store it in an airtight bag. Cartridges keep filtering even when they are not on the face and will lose effectiveness over time.

mask when sanding, carving, cutting, or grinding almost all materials because dust will be produced. The dust could be anything from bead foam to wood particulate but it is still dust and inhalation of any synthetic or organic particle over time is bad for the lungs.

Overall the best mask to use when sanding is still the respirator because, when well fitted, the respirator does not allow any gaps around the face. Gaps or bulges in the rubber face mask, designed to make an airtight seal on the face, can allow particles to bypass the filters, rendering the respirator useless.

Tip

Dust masks should *never* be worn in place of a respirator when there are dangerous gaseous compounds present. In some instances the dust mask can make the situation worse, trapping fumes around the face, and reducing any possibility that fresh air will disperse the fumes.

Low VOC Materials

These products have a reduction of VOC. You will often see "low VOC" or "no VOC" as a description for interior house paints and cleaning products, indicating that the "paint smell" or the "chemical odor", and therefore the possible harmful compounds or vapors, have been reduced or eliminated completely. In the case of foam fabrication, low VOC adhesives have little if any smell and seem very safe to use indoors and get on the skin. But even though it is low VOC these adhesives may still contain small amounts of potentially harmful chemicals. In practical terms you could possibly be exposed to low VOC products for a longer period of time without permanent damage. The no VOC products are the best ones to look for and use.

Note: everyone can have a different reaction to any product, so care should be taken; this means always reading the directions, the MSDS or SDS, becoming familiar with the GHS, using good judgment, and keeping your eyes open.

High VOC Materials

The major drawback with these products (including paint, adhesives, paint removers, dyes, plastics, etc.) is that they contain chemicals that are harmful to inhale and get on the skin (not to mention the ingredients used to make these products and the methods of disposal). A high VOC adhesive must be used in a well-ventilated area such as outside, a cross-ventilated room, or in a ventilated spray booth. In addition, the appropriate gloves and respirator cartridges rated to block the topical chemicals and toxic vapors must be worn. These adhesives are durable and fast drying but use them as a last resort. The chemicals can be absorbed through the skin and the vapors are strong. These have been known to cause neurological and respiratory side effects. Generally there are clear warnings written with the directions—read these and take heed.

Spray Paint

When using spray paint what is happening? You are producing a fine particulate that is diluted with a solvent, which is propelled by an aerosol. I have never used a spray paint that did not have a strong smell or that did not propel paint particles into the air. This is a no-brainer: spray paint is a product that can be easily inhaled contaminating your lungs, blood stream, and brain. Wearing a respirator (even outside) or using a paint booth is a must for products that suspend particles and fumes in the air. Even though you may be using spray paint for only a short blast, the fumes and the particulate will still be floating around until fresh air carries them away.

If using a fan to blow the paint fumes down a hallway in a big building, do not think that you are safe. The fumes are still trapped in the building and you are subjecting yourself and the other building inhabitants to the harmful compounds.

Figure 2-3: When airbrushing paint particulate is suspended in the air.

When using an airbrush, tiny particles (paint, make-up, fixative, etc.) are blown into the air with air pressure. The air is not the problem, but the particulate is. Wear a snug fitting dust mask, or a respirator, and eye protection.

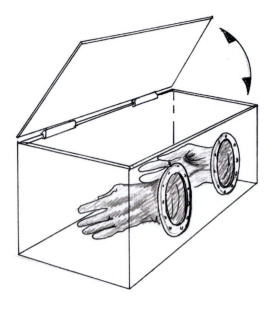

Figure 2-4: Sample of dye-mixing box.

What is Meant by the Term "Gas Off"?

The term "gas off" pertains to vapors still remaining on an object or in an area after the product has dried or gone through its chemical process. Using an item that has not had time to gas off, or dispel the fumes, can be just as harmful as inhaling the active solvents during the application of applying the various products. You do not want an actor to put something on that has not had time to go through this process properly. Nobody wants to be a human chemical filter! If you need to use products that are high VOC then allot drying time for safety.

Dye

Dye is a product that adds color through a chemical reaction. Dyes can be organic or synthetic and can also (if not used carefully) be cumulatively bad for you health. Dye can enter your body through skin, eye, and mucus membrane absorption, and through inhalation in the mouth and nose. Most dyes are in powder form but some come pre-suspended in liquid. Those suspended in liquid are safer in terms of air contamination but gloves and proper clothing should still be worn.

The best way to mix dry dyes is in a chemical mixing box. This can be a wooden and plexi-glass box with a hinged lid. Rubber gloves can be permanently attached to the sides or there might be holes in the sides for gloved hands to slide through. The enclosed box allows for the dye particulate to be mixed into a liquid form inside a controlled space. When mixing is complete the box can be wiped down.

If a mixing box is not available, the next best thing is to use a dust mask, rubber gloves, goggles, and a spray water bottle to spritz the dry dye out of the air. After the dying procedure is finished, wipe down all surfaces during clean-up with a damp cloth. *Note*: this is not ideal and you will still have some exposure to the particulate.

Tip

Never stand over steaming pots of dye; the steam can lift particulate and vapors that can be inhaled and enter the body through the membranes in the eyes, nose, and mouth. Good ventilation is also recommended in this situation.

Paint

When using any paint, common sense tells us that we should not ingest, inhale, rub it on our skin or in our eyes. Some paints may contain silica, toxic pigments such as cadmium, manganese, titanium dioxide, and many other chemicals that are bad for our health.

Skin does a very good job of shielding the body, and there are many paint products that are not necessarily bad unless turned into a form that can enter our bodies. For example, when we suspend a material like latex or acrylic craft paint into particulate when sanding or airbrushing, we have turned it into a form of inhalable paint. Again caution in the form of research and wearing the proper safety equipment is the key. Knowledge is power!

Be aware of the following processes that allow chemicals to enter the body:

- Sanding/grinding/drilling
- Airbrushing
- Spray painting
- Spraying adhesives

- Painting (if it gets on the skin and under fingernails)
- Painting (if paint is swallowed)
- Using chemicals with volatile organic compounds (enter through mouth, skin, nose, eyes).

Tool Awareness

The obvious danger with some electric and hand-held tools is the risk of cutting into or through flesh (and bone), abrading the skin, being hit by flying debris, and inhaling particulate. Many people have fears or even phobias about using electric power tools—perhaps it is the noise or how fast these tools do their job. Just like driving a car, there are inherent risks when using power tools. Accidents nearly always involve misuse, safety errors, or working too quickly.

Suggestions When Using Power Tools

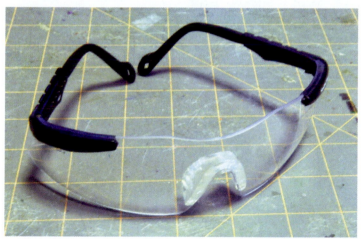

Figure 2-5: Safety glassware: only one example out of dozens of vision protection available.

1. **Wear protective eyewear.** You only have two eyes. Why take a chance on damaging or losing the ability to see? Put

on a pair of goggles or safety glasses. How long does that take?

2. **Wear a dust mask.** When sanding or cutting, dust is always produced. You can carry your own collapsible dust mask in a zip lock bag tucked in your work apron or coverall so it will be handy whenever you need it.

3. **Wear ear protection.** There is the "headphone" variety that covers the whole ear and the foam inserts that go inside the ear. They both work well to help protect your ears from damage. Check the *Noise Reduction Rating* (NRR) on hearing protection to make certain you are getting the maximum protection needed.

Figure 2-6: Ear protection.

blades of the machinery dragging you with it. Generally this happens really fast and if you are not hurt the only recourse is to cut off the hair or the clothing that is caught in the machinery.

4. **Wear sturdy shoes that cover your feet.** Shops will often insist that occupants wear closed-toed shoes. Heavy, sharp tools and materials can fall off tables and crush your very important feet.

5. **Tie up or remove any loose objects such as jewelry, clothing, hair, and keys.** The famous dancer Isadora Duncan thought it would be a great idea to take a ride in a convertible with her long, loose scarves blowing in the wind behind her. Unfortunately one of these scarves wrapped around a rear wheel and her neck was broken. Loose items can easily be caught up and dragged into the wheels and

6. **Know where the "on/off" switch is located and if there is a safety shut off.** If there is a problem you may get a few lucky seconds to shut off the machine before damage is done. Commit the location of the switch to memory and even go through the motions of turning it off. Practice can imprint muscle memory and help with reflex actions.

7. **Know how your material will react to what's being done to it.** Foam, for example, will sometimes get caught or grabbed by the belt sander popping up and out of your grip. It can make a loud "pop" and be very sudden and surprising. The only way to know how the machine will react to the material is to do a sample test first. The goal is to try and eliminate any possible surprises that might happen.

8. **Know basic first aid and emergency procedures.** How do you treat a deep cut or a small amputation (a severed fingertip)? Where is the first aid kit located? Is there an eyewash station? What is the procedure for serious medical emergencies? All of this information should be in the back of your mind before you use tools that can damage you physically.

9. **Know where power cords are located, and what's on the back of the item being cut.** If using hand-held power tools the power cord can sometimes get in the way and is easily cut through. The same goes for cutting surfaces supporting your material. Tables have been hacked into and saw horses cut apart because the entire workspace was not taken into consideration.

Figure 2-7: Eyewash station.

"An ounce of prevention is worth a pound of cure" is a very well-known proverb that can apply specifically to safety. Spend a few minutes making sure everything is safe and set up properly, and hopefully you will not need to spend six months in a cast or several years receiving repeated corrective eye surgery.

Remember: you are in charge of your own safety. In this case "ignorance is not bliss, it is just ignorance" and can be very dangerous.

chapter three

what type of foam to use?

The Needs of the Project

There are several options when considering what sort of foam is best for the project. One way to start the decision process is to ask yourself the needs of the project.

Questions to ask:

1. How big will the item be?
2. Will it be covered or painted?
3. How will you build it—by building up layers and carving or by relying mostly on the patterned skin?
4. How will it move?
5. Does it need to be flexible?
6. How durable does it need to be?
7. How long is your construction period?

Remember there are no rules when working with foam. Just as long as the finished product meets all the design requirements, it is possible to use any foam and any foam building technique to build up and carve or pattern the desired shape.

Closed-Cell Foam/L 200

L 200 has become standard use for many costume and puppet applications.

When joined together to make shapes, especially larger shapes, L 200 seems to be more structural and able to support itself better than other foams. I also lean more towards using closed-cell foam because it weighs so little. If a puppet will be held over the operator's head for long periods of time or if it is a costume character that is worn, closed-cell foam is the best choice.

If I were planning to use paint as a finish and I wanted the texture to be smooth, slimy, hard, or shiny, I would definitely choose L 200. Again this is also a good foam for carving and sanding and you can get a lot of realistic detail. Painting the surface with acrylic or latex paints is very effective. Even if it is not sealed the foam absorbs the pigment and brushes on very well. You need to work fast, but the end result is smooth and as realistic or fantastic as you need it to be.

When using thicker L 200 to pattern a shell (1 inch or more), the thicker foam is sometimes harder to encourage to

Meet Mr. Brick!

Closed-Cell, Open-Cell, or Rigid Foam?

Table 3.1

Carving	Patterned	Sanding	Weight	Can be sewn	Can be cast in a mold	Dyeable	Paintable	Shaped with heat	Natural color
scissors, sharp blades, bandsaw	yes	belt sander	lightweight	machine or by hand	no	yes	yes	no	off-white
scissors, sharp blades, carving knife	yes	somewhat—belt sander	mediumweight	no	no	yes	yes	no	off-white, green, pink
scissors, sharp blades, bandsaw	yes	belt sander, sandpaper	lightweight	no	no	no	yes	yes	white, black, multi
rasps, saws, all blades, hot wire tools, knives, lathes	no	rasps, belt sander, sandpaper	lightweight	no	no	no	if coated	no	white
sharp blades, bandsaw, hand saw	no	rasps, belt sander, sandpaper	lightweight	no	no	no	If coated	no	pink, blue, and green
sharp blades, bandsaw, hand saw	no	belt sander, sandpaper, files	mediumweight	no	yes	no	can be intrinsically colored	no	off-white/ yellow
razor blades, scissors	no	no	mediumweight	no	yes	no	can be intrinsically colored	no	off-white/ yellow
scissors, hand saw, razor blades	no	belt sander, coarse sandpaper	light- to mediumweight	no	no	no	after covered or coated	no	gray, white, multi

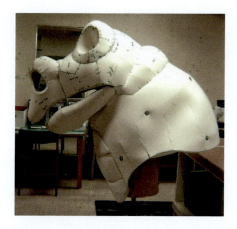

Figure 3-1: George the T-Rex in process.

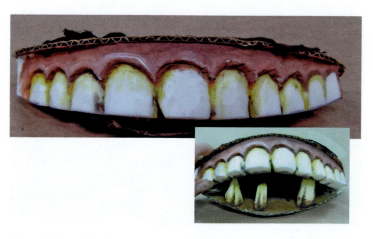

Figure 3-2: Sample teeth made of painted L 200.

make small, tight, detailed shapes. If relying strictly on the *patterned shape* to make tight turns and contours, consider varying the thickness of the foam or construct with the knowledge that you will be custom-carving the details. The thinner foam will not be as structural but it will allow for more tight contours and versatility.

If the foundation structure is made of thick foam (1/2 inch to 1 inch) any non-structural details such as wrinkles can be made of thinner material (1/8 inch to 1/4 inch) and added on top.

It is also possible to glue slabs of thick L 200 together to make a solid block that can be carved and sanded (Figure 3-4).

A.

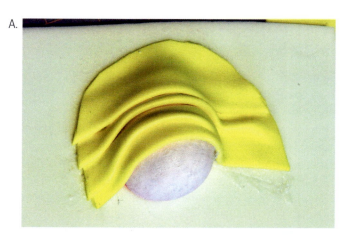

B.

Figure 3-3: Adding gathered layers of thin L 200 for a wrinkled effect.
A. 1/8-inch sheet of yellow L 200. Add contact adhesive to the back. As it crimps and folds, it will stick to itself.
B. Sample with finish paint.

A.

B.

C.

Figure 3-4:

A. Glued layers of L 200 being carved. Stacked 1-inch foam with toe sketched on the side.

B. Toe cut out on the band saw then sanded on the belt sander.

C. Finished toe with details.

This might be used for a very tall rod puppet held overhead or as part of a bigger costume such as that used for the *King* or *Queen Carnivale* celebration (Figure 3-5).

Open-Cell Urethane Foam: Reticulated

This foam can be shaped with scissors and razor blades. In terms of flexibility, being able to sew into the foam, and finishing the foam by dyeing, reticulated foam (*open*-cell urethane foam) is your best bet. I use this material for puppets, and fat suits (open-cell *upholstery* or polyether foam is the cheapest and easiest to find and can make very nice fat suits too!). It is also lightweight, comes in different thicknesses, and is very flexible and durable. In addition to finishing with fur or fabric, this foam can also be left uncovered to be painted, sanded, and carved. The small pores will always be there (which for many projects is very desirable); therefore the finish will never be absolutely smooth as with L 200.

A.

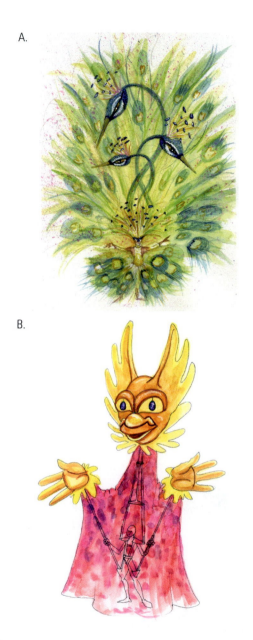

B.

Figure 3-6: The surface finish when using raw reticulated foam.

Figure 3-5:
A. Carnivale costume design.
B. Giant rod puppet design.

Open-Cell Urethane Foam: Upholstery Grade

Many foam artisans use *open-cell upholstery grade foam* to produce really wonderful masks, puppets, costumes, and props. It carves well with electric knives, razor blades, and scissors—it is possible to get quite a nice level of carved detail too. In terms of finishing, it takes spray paint and airbrushes very smoothly. The only drawback is that it is not as strong as the reticulated foam and it has a shorter life/use expectancy. It will become brittle and fragile with extended use and can sag.

However, there are some artisans who have kept items made with upholstery foam for years. It should be finished with a fabric or latex skin and kept out of sunlight when it is stored. Exposure to moisture such as sweat will compromise its structure even more quickly. When I spend a lot of time building a project, I want a material that I know will last for as long as possible so I veer away from using upholstery foam for permanent projects. I generally end up using upholstery grade foam only for mock-ups.

Figure 3-7: Bubo the Roman Clown. Urethane upholstery foam and airbrush.

Rigid Foam

For *foam patterning* rigid foam is primarily used for the positive sculpt. When the sculpt is carved and shaped, a thin layer of material such as fabric or tape and plastic is contoured over it and the pattern is developed from there. See *Chapters 6–8*.

I prefer to use rigid foam for finished carvings that may end up moving by adding hinged joints. The joints can be constructed of fabric, leather, or metal hinges. The foam surface would be sealed to add durability and then painted with a brush, airbrush, or sponge. It can also be covered with faux fur or fabric.

It is very useful for detail pieces such as the bear's nose. Blue extruded polystyrene or polyethylene foam can be sculpted and sanded then covered with scrap fabric and glue. When dry, layers of *Sculpt Or Coat* can be successively stippled over it, applied with a scrap of reticulated foam (Figure 3-8).

Again there are no rules or limits. Take and chance and have fun!

Figure 3-8: Bear's nose sculpted out of extruded polystyrene foam and covered with fabric and glue.

A flower is born!

SECTION II

DESIGN

chapter four

an approach to design

This chapter touches on different methodologies and ways to produce a design. It will also discuss working drawings, and how to begin translating a design into a three-dimensional object. The primary aim is towards those artists who create designs for story-telling in performance venues such as theater, television, and film, but there are many forms of art to which this could apply.

How does this chapter pertain to patterning foam? The simple answer is that part of the fun and success of creating is building an object that is interesting, that provokes thought, and is pleasing to the eye. A good way to start is to design the object first solving the two-dimensional challenges before attempting to scrabble around in three dimensions. Working without a design or image is not the *wrong way*; there is no wrong way when it comes to creation. Many artisans work by creating as they go. Committing to a design is the first step towards creating a three-dimensional object and it is a part of the planning process, especially when factors such as budgeting, collaborating with other artists, and sorting out technical challenges weigh heavy on the project.

There are two fundamental ways to approach a design:

1. **focusing only on the design**, i.e. thinking about and creating the object, creature, scenic, lighting, sound, or costume design, etc. as if you are living in the world where it exists;

2. **simultaneously creating the design and how it is built**, i.e. figuring out all the materials and under structures as the concept is being created.

Both approaches are valid and most designers will eventually want to have some input on *what* makes the texture, the materials needed to construct it, and functionality, among other things.

Approach 1: Solving the "What"

The first design approach is really wide open and is perhaps an intimidating way to work for some beginning and even experienced designers. It's very important with this method to not solve the problem of *how* it is made until you can think of it as a *being* or a *real thing*. In other words can you see it, smell it, and lean against it mentally? This approach involves constantly questioning, filling your head with essential images, ideas, impressions, and using your imagination.

Often we are very anchored in the physical world, and what we see every day is what is stuck in our mind. It could be called a mental rut. This is one really good reason to do research.

Needless to say designers of all levels should inundate their brains with colors, ideas, textures, silhouettes, impressions, artists, objects etc. so that all the raw information can be filed away and mentally churned. A good friend once said to me that "[the act of researching] is a mental tilling-of-the-earth".

It is important to note that *research* does not necessarily need to be "on" the subject we are aiming for. In fact it is very often helpful in the initial design stage to read and look at random images that do not pertain to the subject at all. This can lead down unexpected paths, jostling the mind in a different direction. When in the "mental design zone", designers can become an "idea conduit" and the oddest things can *affect* and *infect* them; the angle of a table leg, how a dog's ear flaps, or the impression a boot sole makes in the snow can take a designer to other places.

Equally as important as collecting mental information is imagination. Being able to project yourself *into* the world of the design. It is a bit like a child's game, and playing pretend. It is a way of seeing the reality of the design. Begin by thinking everything is a *real thing* within its reality, be it costume, puppet, or prop. In your mind's eye see how the evening light plays across it, how it moves, breathes, talks, the smell of it as it walks by you, etc.; in short, think of the prop, character, scenery, and even light and sound in the three-dimensional environment where it exists.

A style, a time period, and a season may already have been chosen for the world; let these elements lead and influence the creation of the design. For example, if a script calls for a chair from an environment that is twisted, dark, and stifling begin by looking around at the atmosphere and characters in the world (Figure 4-1). Is it a dank, foggy place with dim light? Who sits on the chair? Who built it? Were they a clever craftsperson? Was it built from the remains of past court advisors? And so on. Let the imagination play with color, shape, scale, and texture, without solving the problem of what it is really constructed from, what sort of paint will be used, whether it will need to be danced on and therefore how sturdy it should be. All of these are valid questions but the type of paint and how much is needed should not usually concern the designer, until they have decided on the mood and line.

Figure 4-1

Sometimes solving the *how* before or simultaneously with the *what* can fundamentally inhibit the designer or the design. It is after all the designer's job to create the *look*. And when you think about it, creating something from the inside out seems counterintuitive. Inventors are always thinking about the purpose or the use of an item before they get into the nitty gritty of materials and cost. People or audiences looking at a finished design can only see the outside surface, and if it doesn't look right or make sense then the design has failed. The design has to be pleasing to the eye, or freakishly terrifying, or off-kilter in some way as dictated by the world where it exists, or it will seem distracting and wrong.

Many designers are often expected to solve the construction challenges and even build what they design, but the physical construction should not dictate the design unless it is visually a part of the design.

If you are unused to transporting yourself mentally to another place when you design, challenge yourself when next designing anything (a character, a scenic piece, a costume, or a prop). Try not to think about what it will be made of or how it will be made. Instead simply design it the way it should look, and after you are satisfied, then start thinking about how to make it. If you are in the habit of thinking about how to make a thing as you design it, it might prove difficult at first, but I find that this exercise can be really liberating. The more you practice the more you will free your imagination as an artist.

Approach 2: Solving the "How" with the "What"

The second approach or "designing by deciding the *how* along with the *what*" is commonly practiced on tight deadlines and when the designer is in a dual role—that of being both the designer and the construction expert. Depending on the director and the needs of the production, this process can be effective. Many wonderful designs have been produced this way. However, it can sometimes take the enjoyment out of what we do and unconsciously (or consciously) limit creativity by requiring the designer to sit in two worlds at once. This technique involves not only knowing the world of the design, but also the practical aspects of the design simultaneously. A knowledge of your stock, your budget, and what might be available to purchase is also helpful when using this method.

The Elements of Design

Line and Form

I feel strongly that of all the elements of design (line, color, texture, form, etc.) *line* and *form* are two of the most important when determining the *attitude* or *flavor* of the character, scenery, or prop. A straight line versus a slanting line, or a curved line versus a squiggly line—it is exciting to think that a mere line can create a mood or a feeling.

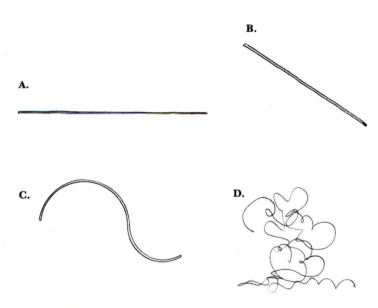

Figure 4-2: The different attitudes of a line.
A. Steady, dependable, boring, stable.
B. Askew, off-kilter, unsteady, tense.
C. Introspective, relaxed, determined.
D. Whimsical, chaotic, happy, free, unmanageable.

Form is equally as important. A box with straight, symmetrical sides looks stiff, proper, and upright in contrast to a box with asymmetrical, curved sides—it looks deflated, mashed, and irregular.

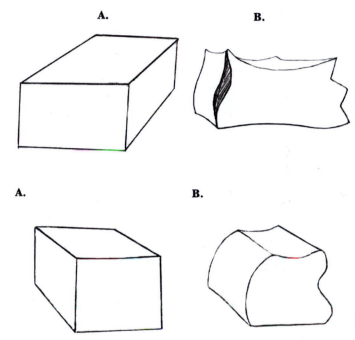

Figure 4-3: Variations on form.

With these two basic elements, a very mundane object can take on a different persona or mood.

Texture

Texture is absolutely one of my most favorite design elements. Yes, line and form can tell you about the attitude and mass of the object, but the details of depth and surface treatment can make a design seem very real and give it a richness that mere line and form cannot. As mentioned previously it is helpful to make a list of descriptive adjectives when mentally creating the

A.

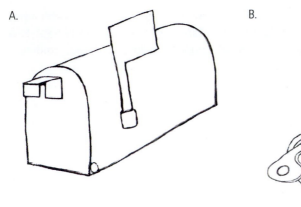

B.

C.

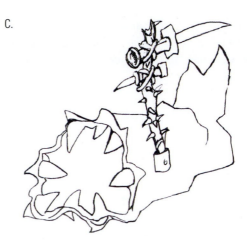

Figure 4-4: Designs of a practical item with three looks using line and form:

A. Realistic.

B. Whimsical.

C. Dangerous.

character or object. For example, words can suggest different textures:

1. **Organic**—soft, bumpy, slimy, furry, rough, scaly, scabby, hairy, pimply.
2. **Man-made**—hard, smooth, frictionless, sharp, reflective, plastic, sterile.

A.

B.

Figure 4-6:

A. Character drawn with only shape and line.

B. Same character with added texture.

Figure 4-5: Samples of different textures.

Color

Color is one of the more powerful elements of design that can have a very strong emotional and personal effect on an audience. It can be associated with national pride, emotions, sexual attraction, seasons, status, traditional ceremonies, etc., and these associations can vary greatly in every country and with every person. In addition it is important when discussing color that there is a visual sample used as a reference—just mentioning the color blue in conversation, for example, could be taken to mean any number of shades or tints (Figure 4-7).

The color *scheme* is a way to unify or define a design with color. The various color combinations, whether it be the bright and jangling *complementary scheme* or the mellow and nonintrusive *neutral scheme*, can have a huge impact on a design and help set the mood or feeling.

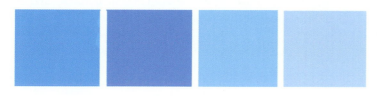

Figure 4-7: Samples of "sky" blue.

Techniques to Help Inspire and Shape a Design

Here are a few suggestions to help organize and shape the design process.

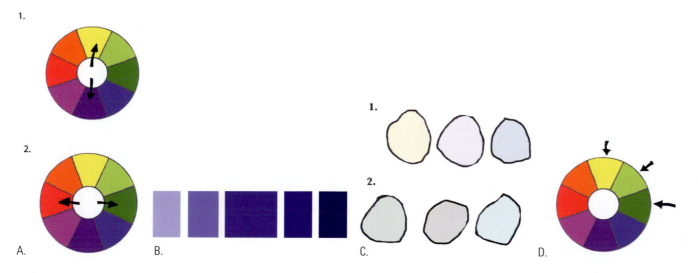

Figure 4-8: Color schemes.

A. Complementary—color combination that sits opposite on the color wheel. When these colors stand together they are vibrant but when mixed the color combination is gray.

B. Monochromatic—one color that shows variations in light and dark.

C. Neutral—a color scheme that is pale, muted, and lacks contrast.

D. Analogous—colors that sit side by side on the color wheel in groups of three.

1. **Make a list of adjectives.** The list is a very good way to begin to break down or define the *mood* of a story or play. Ask: How does this make you feel? What is the color and texture of this particular sadness or happiness? And so forth.

2. **Research.** As mentioned earlier in the chapter, research can provide us with the foundation information and raw material for feeding our ideas. It is most definitely "food for thought".

3. **Making a collage.** This may seem like a very rudimentary exercise, but for a designer selecting images and colors and arranging them on a panel is the equivalent of free writing for a writer. It gets all the images out there in one space for the eye and brain to take in at once.

4. **Color samples and mini plots.** Some designers begin by laying out color chips or swatches to get a sense of the arc of the whole show or object. This can also be done by drawing *mini plots* using characters, light cones, or scenic sketches—no more detailed than stick figures or crude shapes—that illustrate how the color and silhouette changes as time passes. Both are handy techniques.

A.

B.

Figure 4-9:

A. Color samples from the production of *Dracula*.

B. Mini plot for scene from *Mary Poppins*.

5. **Thumbnail sketches.** After the preliminary research, collage, and color samples have been reviewed, *thumbnail sketches* are the next step towards crystalizing a design. The term refers to sketches that are quick and varied to capture an initial idea and are crucial in the process when showing how all the research and translation of ideas are forming in to a single look.

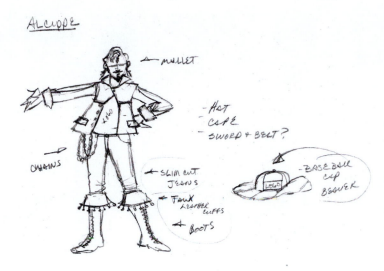

Figure 4-10: An example of thumbnail sketches.

Tim Burton comes to mind. He has a very distinct look that comes through in most of his films. When you see images of some scenic or costume designs sometimes you can tell, "Oh, that looks like so-an-so's work." Or, "That looks like a *copy* of so-and-so's work."

This is separate from what can be called *industrial* or *cosmetic* design. This type of designer creates a style of objects such as clothing or furniture. In this case the "style" or "commercial line" of items is what makes it attractive and marketable. Designers who create for entertainment utilize these different styles of clothing, furniture, and music to enhance the story. These items are the entertainment designer's foundation material.

6. **Mental flexibility.** Perhaps the most important and healthiest quality to possess as a designer is the ability and willingness to move in a variety of artistic directions as needed by the process. This ability will also allow you to follow an impulse or idea and see where it can take you.

A Note on "Style"

One of the big challenges for the designer is to try and remove their own personal preferences from the equation such as trying not to have a favorite color, or "style". Traditionally for entertainment, it is not about the designer's personal expression and preference; it is about the needs of the design.

Conversely, of course, there are designers who have a style, which makes them identifiable. The director and designer

chapter five

renderings, working drawings, and simplicity of form

Visual Tools

Color Renderings

The purpose of the color rendering can be twofold. The primary purpose is to be used as a resource or a map for determining the scale, color, texture, etc. of the realized design. However, it can also be used as a piece of *concept art* to help illustrate the mood of a show, communicating the atmosphere or the

Why is it important for a designer to produce a design rendering and include *working drawings*? Designs are often only the first step in the long process of creating a tangible, three-dimensional object. *One* rendering of a single view gives only *one* window of information, albeit very helpful information. Often it is very easy to forget that the construction crew is not quivering with anticipation in the designer's head, intuitively knowing exactly what is needed. It is a designer's job to provide a solution for every visual detail so that the construction crew does not need to waste time solving the aesthetic challenges. There are, however, those crafts-people who want, expect, and even appreciate receiving *suggestive designs* so that they can interpret and bring what the designer has drawn into the real world. These artisans may know, for example, what fabrics or plastics might give the needed "translucency and spring" to a design. Needless to say there are designers who specialize in props, costumes, scenery, make-up, lighting, costume crafts, wigs, hats—the list goes on and on—but generally all of these will provide an image of some sort to communicate their ideas towards interpretation and construction of the finished design.

Figure 5-1: Example of a design that could be used as concept art.

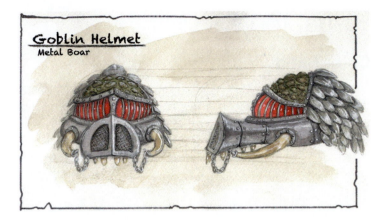

Figure 5-2: Example of a design for a goblin helmet.

interpretation of character. This can be communicated in the way the drawing is presented. Presentation style can be enhanced with a painted background, drawn in a style emulating a certain artist, and/or with a title block with a special graphic.

The color rendering should be able to communicate the desired design as accurately and as fluidly as possible. Below is a list of what a color rendering should communicate:

1. **Scale.** If the design is for a chair, a window, or a pair of clown shoes, then how big will these need to be? To illustrate scale in an initial presentation rendering, it is very helpful to include a human form either standing in the scene or wearing the costume. If the costume is something that distorts the human form, then it is helpful to include in the working drawings an interior sketch of how the body "fits" or "lines up" inside the character.

2. **Suggestion of color and texture.** Sometimes renderings might include color and texture on only half of the drawing, especially if there are a large number of designs and the design is extremely complicated. Whether fully or partially fleshed out, the rendering has achieved its purpose if it communicates *what* goes *where*.

3. **Swatches and samples.** When creating design renderings it is traditional and very helpful to attach small swatches to indicate the fabrics and where they will be used. If there are a lot of fabrics requiring manipulation in a special way to create unique textures, these can be displayed on separate panels or "craft boards".

4. **Title plate.** A clear title plate, which includes the name of the production, and any additional titles or labels that may be relevant to the design such as character, act, scene, etc. should be placed in the same spot on all renderings for easy access.

5. **Movement.** If movement is a critical part of a design such as with dance or large-scale puppetry, then some suggestion or acknowledgment of how the fabrics or costume might move is informative.

6. **Suggestion of fabric fullness.** If dealing with fabric, and it is expected a lot of fabric will be used in curtains or clothing, then some sense of how full they are will help with future planning and budgeting.

7. **Rear view.** A small rear-view sketch can be included on the color rendering. These are especially helpful when communicating the details of a three-dimensional object. Sometimes these are included on separate panels.

Style Sheets

The style sheet is an extremely helpful design tool. Its purpose is to support the finished design by helping to further illustrate specific details. One or more style sheets can include: collage images of research, sketches, color swatches, etc. It differs from the *research collage* mentioned in *Chapter 4* in that the *style sheet* is specific to a character or object and its design. The artisan can turn to the style sheet as a specific, focused tool to help with interpreting a design.

Working Drawings

After the design is complete, *working drawings* are the next step. These will include profile views, detailed sketches of

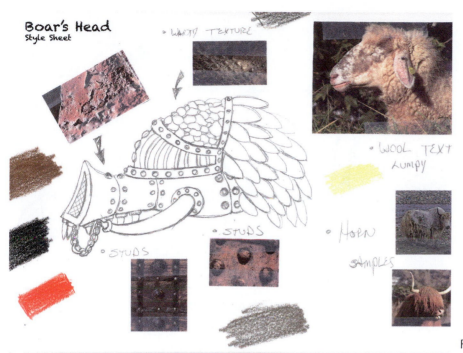

Figure 5-3: Example of a supporting style sheet.

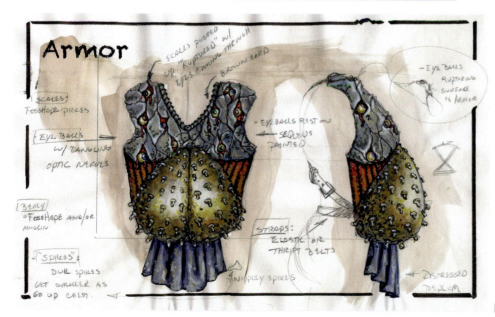

Figure 5-4: A design with notes.

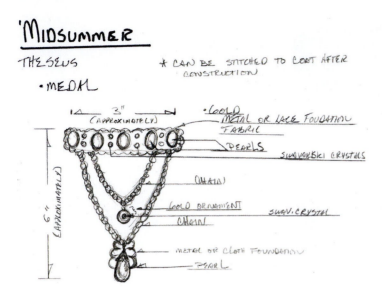

Figure 5-5: Examples of a working drawing.

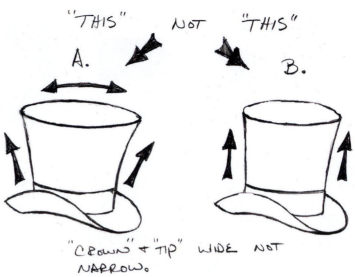

Figure 5-6: This note might be used on sample animation boards for character designs or when a theatrical design is sent out to a shop to be made.

specific areas (showing how a part fits together), or where a visible seam or joint (placed for aesthetic purposes) might need to be.

Some of these drawings might include sketches of how the item should *not* look.

If working drawings are provided it is extremely important to read them through, make lists, and ask questions. The designer has taken the time to solve all the visual details and therefore care should be taken by the artisan and craftsperson to follow their lead.

Detail Drawings

Detail drawings, whether they are drafted or hand drawn, are provided to help explain any tangible construction challenges. This can include any support materials created on a computer or by hand to further illustrate and break down details.

Detail drawings should include:

1. Title plate.
2. Neatly written notes and descriptions.
3. Profile views. (Profile views are those drawings that provide different points of view of an object. These are necessary to get the whole sense and look of the object or space in three dimensions.)
4. Mention of materials if desired.
5. Measurements and scale references.
6. References and referrals pertaining to other departments such as movement, lighting, scenic, costume, and sound.

Profile views

A.

B.

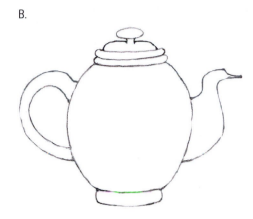

C.

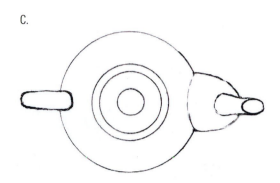

Figure 5-7: Different angles of presentation.

A. Front view.

B. Side view.

C. Plan view.

A.

B.

C.

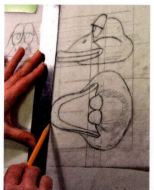

D.

Figure 5-8: The procedure to develop a dimensional profile of a character.

A. Sample character.

B. Laying out support lines of side view or profile.

C. Fleshing out side view.

D. Laying out support lines of plan view or top view.

Paring Down the Object to Its Foundation Shape

Working drawings might also include a sketch of an object's *foundation shape* (Figure 5-9). If a design is very complicated or covered with a thick finish layer, it is important to pare down the shape into a more simplistic form to help the artisan or craftsman understand the foundation. This is especially important when working on a project that has a lot of detail and dimensional texture. Sometimes the foundation is obscured by all the activity and frenzy of the surface detail. A good tool to help with this type of drawing is a light box. If a light box is not available then a bright window is just as handy (Figure 5-10).

Figure 5-9: A detail sketch and the pared-down foundation shape.

A.
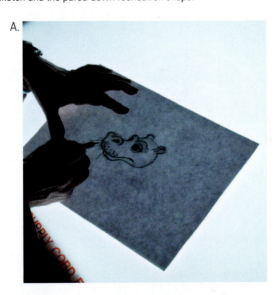

B.
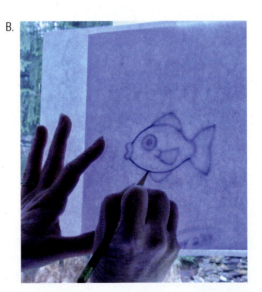

Figure 5-10
A. Using a light box.   B. Using a bright window.

SECTION III

TRANSLATING DESIGN INTO REALITY: TECHNIQUES USED IN THE PATTERNING PROCESS

chapter six

additive patterning:
adding a surface layer

The next four chapters cover different techniques used to create custom foam patterns and shapes. These methods include: the *additive* and *subtractive* methods as well as *speed patterning* and the *free-form* construction process. The majority of these techniques start with a model, a positive sculpt or a maquette that is used as a form of mannequin from which to pattern. Keep in mind that there are loads of variations on these techniques and that there is no "right way" of working with foam. The only right way is the process that you are comfortable working with and that achieves the finished product you desire.

The Additive Foam Patterning Process

Additive patterning is a term that I use to describe techniques that *add* a surface layer or "skin" to a *positive sculpt* or *maquette*. It involves starting with a form, adding a skin to it, and cutting the skin away to make the pattern. This is the same technique utilized by garment drapers using a dress form or mannequin as a foundation to apply a "fabric skin". The dress form, padded into the desired shape and size, is covered with a fabric skin, the pattern shapes are drawn onto the fabric skin, removed, spread flat, and cut into shapes, thus making a pattern (Figure 6-1).

Wig makers use a similar technique to pattern a model's head when making a custom wig. The model's head is covered/wrapped with plastic and tape (Figure 6-2). The resulting plastic-and-tape skin is pulled away, padded, and blocked on a head form. It is then used as the foundation on which to contour the ventilating lace with the end result being a custom wig.

Steps for Additive Foam Patterning

1. **The design.** It is helpful to have all the profile sketches decided and the shape pared down to reveal the foundation before beginning to sculpt. Make enlarged copies of the sketches and the finished design, and position them around your working space so you can see them while working. Although a laptop and an iPhone are handy tools, having to revive them every time you need to glance at the very small screen image or stopping to search and find the one piece of missing research you need interrupts the process and takes the focus away from what you are working on.

2. **The positive sculpt.** Additive patterning involves creating a sculpture or *positive*. The positive can be made of any firm material you feel comfortable working with and that best captures your idea. The options may include: potter's clay, plasticine, rigid foam (polystyrene or rigid urethane), or compressed paper and tape.

   When using clay, both plasticine and potter's clay are good mediums in which to sculpt a positive. Clay is my first choice because of the detailed and accurate interpretation of the design that can be achieved, and the ease with which the sculpt can be modified. However, if the shapes are simple and I need a quick pattern to move forward, I will use "compressed paper and tape" to get the shape that is needed.

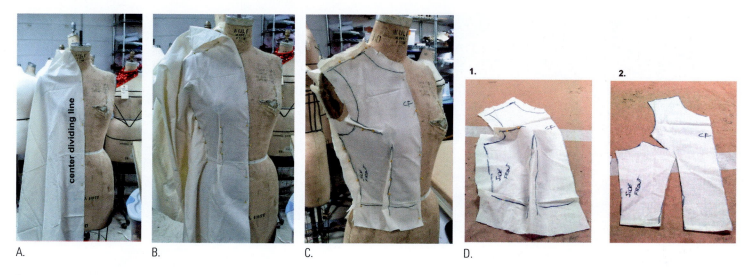

A.   B.   C.   D.

Figure 6-1: Draping a mannequin.

A. Laying on fabric at center dividing line.

B. Pinning darts to contour it to the positive shape.

C. Adding notations and notches.

D. Laying the piece out flat to get the pattern.

A.   B.   C.

Figure 6-2: Patterning a model's head for wig making.

A. Draping the plastic.

B. Adding the tape to hold the shape.

C. Taking off the plastic and tape skin to get the pattern.

Figure 6-3: Student Andrew Swisher displays his fighting rooster positive sculpt on a stand.

You can build a positive of any size, ranging from partial scale to the exact size of the finished object. I find, however, that if the finished object is going to be very large it is more efficient (in time, and space) to build a positive that is smaller in scale than the actual size of the finished original. See *Chapters 12–14* for scaling patterns.

Note: if you are new to the process, begin by designing and sculpting a form that is simplistic (Figure 6-5). Try a shape that does not have a lot of contours. Remember a wonderfully complicated and detailed positive sculpt is just that, "complicated and detailed", and it will probably overwhelm the beginner. However, simple shapes can be patterned cleanly and neatly, and then enhanced by adding additional foam pieces for detail.

A.

B.

Figure 6-4: Different examples of positive sculpts.

A. Potter's clay sculpture of a dinosaur.

B. Compressed paper and tape sculpture of a pelican head.

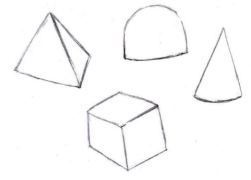

Figure 6-5: Start by learning to pattern simple shapes.

Figure 6-6: A simple shape versus a complicated one.

Figure 6-7: Calipers are a handy tool for measuring. See *Chapter 13*.

A.

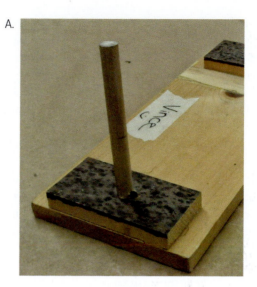

B.

Tip

Take the time to make a stand. If possible find or make a stand on which to sculpt. This will allow you to move the item around evenly at eye level and will give you a way to keep it supported while working. Construct a stand out of scrap plywood, two inch by four inch wood blocks, and a dowel rod or broom handle (Figure 6-8). A threaded pipe and flange bolted to a piece of wood works really well too. Whatever kind of stand it turns out to be, make certain it is stable or you will be constantly fighting to keep it upright while trying to sculpt.

Figure 6-8:
A. Wooden stand.
B. Illustration of a pipe stand.

3. **Adding a skin.** After the positive sculpt is finished, add a covering to create the "skin". The skin may be fabric, plastic wrap and tape, latex, flexible neoprene, etc. Many materials can be used provided they can be made to contour over and around the shapes on the positive sculpt. Whatever final material is used should hug the sculpt "like a skin on a grape". Any bubbles or wrinkles in the applied skin that have malformed the overall shape should be removed or compressed (Figure 6-9).

   • **Fabric skins.** When draping fabric as a skin material the process requires the use of darts to contour the material around the form. Darts are v-shaped tucks pinched into the fabric. The two layers that are pinched are pinned to hold the contour.

   • **Plastic wrap and tape skin.** It is possible to use lightweight plastic grocery bags or vegetable bags from the supermarket because these can contour very well with tape. Lay the plastic on the sculpt. Start at the top and work down. As it sticks to the plastic, the tape will lock the shape in place.

   • **Rubber skin.** Slip casting latex and thin liquid neoprene are both great materials for making a contoured skin. Apply with a sponge or brush. Dried latex and neoprene will stick to itself so new applicators are suggested for additional layers. Allow each layer to dry to the touch before adding the next. Shoot for three to four layers to get a good thickness.

4. **Determining the pattern lines** (Figure 6-10). The accomplished foam pattern maker can create amazing shapes by knowing where the pattern pieces should be laid out on the form and how to cut the pieces with bevels and darts. The use of bevels and darts will be further explained in *Chapter 15*.

   The second part of this process involves adding notes and notches to show where the pieces fit together. This step may seem superfluous but when you cut apart the patterns and lay them out flat, the pieces will be difficult to discern and assemble unless properly annotated.

5. **Remove the skin** (Figure 6-11). When the shapes, notes, and labels have been laid out, the drawn shapes are then

A.

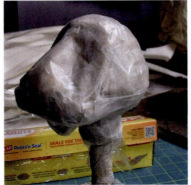

B.

C.

Figure 6-9: Various "skin" coverings:
A. Fabric draping.
B. Plastic wrap and tape.
C. Latex rubber tinted with paint.

A.

B.

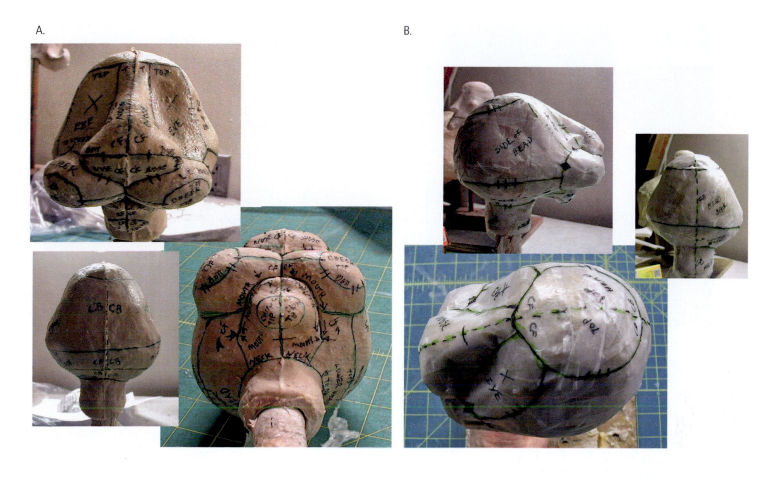

Figure 6-10: Pattern lines and notations added to same clay sculpt with different skin coverings.

A. Latex skin.

B. Plastic wrap and tape skin.

A.

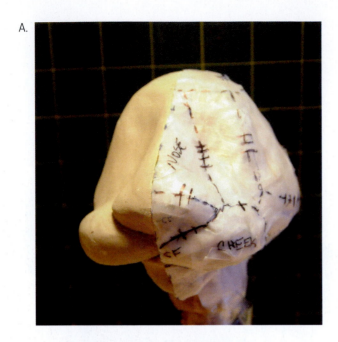

B.

Figure 6-11A and B: Half of a skin removed and then cut apart.

cut away. This will require a pair of small, sharp scissors, also keep an x-acto knife and razor blades on hand for tricky angles.

Cut and remove the skin from an entire half of the object, then carefully cut apart the individual pieces. *Note*: it is a good idea to flatten and tape down the pieces with any additional notes as you go through this process as it is very easy to lose track of which piece goes where and misplace a critical piece.

The next three chapters will cover other patterning methods and challenges. See *Section IV* for the next step in creating the final foam form.

chapter seven

subtractive patterning: cutting away the surface layer

The Subtractive Foam Patterning Process

Subtractive foam patterning is, needless to say, the opposite of *additive foam patterning* in that the skin is not *added* but instead *the surface layer or "skin" is cut away from the positive*. Because of its durability, the suggested foam to use to carve the positive is *reticulated urethane foam*. After the positive has been sculpted, the *center dividing line* and the *pattern divisions* are drawn, then the top-most layer or skin on the sculpt is cut away to produce the patterns. Subtractive patterning is a very precise process needing careful and patient cutting skills. I have used it on several projects and this technique, though painstaking, can produce wonderfully accurate and beautiful pieces.

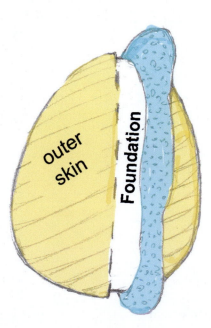

Figure 7-1

Steps for Subtractive Foam Patterning

Again, when learning to pattern foam, the key is to keep your positive sculpt relatively simple (sculpting is the easy part!), and allow plenty of time for experimentation. This is not a process that can be rushed or put off to the last minute.

1. **The design.** Again it is helpful to have all the profile sketches decided and the shape pared down to see the foundation. See the example of the lamp fish design (Figure 7-2). This includes the color rendering and the working drawings to be used as reference while sculpting.

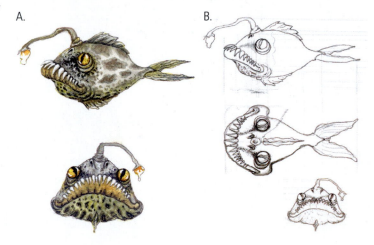

A.

B.

Figure 7-2:
A. Lamp fish design and working drawings.
B. Side, plan, and front views.

2. **The positive sculpt.** The positive sculpture for this method is made from flexible foam such as reticulated urethane foam. Reticulated urethane foam is durable and easy to cut. Using a copy machine, begin by scaling (reducing or enlarging) the design front view and side view to the desired size of the positive. This will create a custom stencil (Figure 7-3).

Then after finding a piece of reticulated foam that is thick enough in height and width to accommodate your stencils, transfer the front view by tracing it with a sharpie (Figure 7-4). You will notice that the porous material makes it a bit harder to draw on than the smoother skins of latex and plastic wrap.

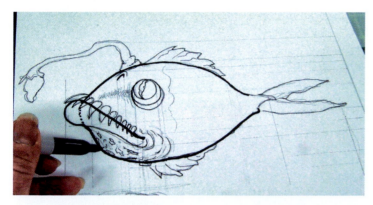

A.

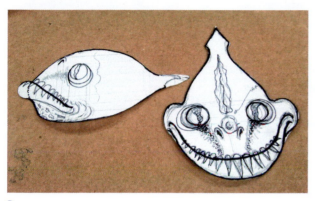

B.

Figure 7-3: Create a custom stencil.
A. Paring down the shape.
B. Profile and front stencils.

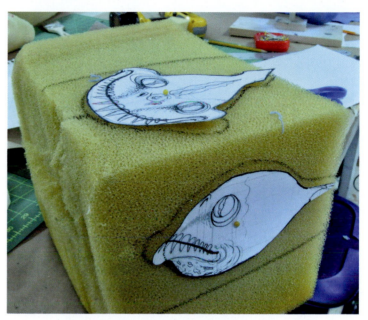

Figure 7-4: Transferring stencils to block foam.

Tip

If you draw a center dividing line you can cut out half of the silhouette and place it on the foam for tracing. Then flip the pattern to get a symmetrical tracing.

Tip

For sculpting with reticulated foam, try and buy this foam with a smaller amount of PPI (pores per square inch)—smaller pores will make transferred lines and notches easier to read.

Line up the side view with the first drawing and trace this side.

Figure 7-5: Cutting out with the band saw.

After the two profile views have been transferred, use a band saw to cut them out (Figure 7-5). After one side has been cut, keep the scrap pieces in place to stabilize the cutting of the second side.

When the rough form has been cut out, use a pair of small, sharp scissors and/or a razor blade to carve out the contours (Figure 7-6). You can hold the positive sculpt in your hand while working, a stand is not required. While modifying the sculpt, make certain you keep turning the

shape in different directions to get as many points of view as possible.

Note: again keep in mind that a simple shape is easier to pattern than a complex one. However, a simple shape can

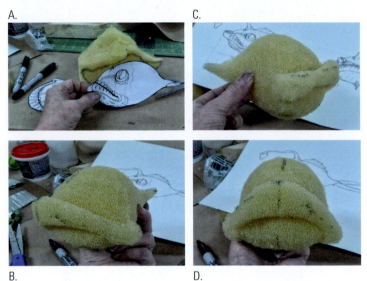

A.   C.

B.   D.

Figure 7-6A–D: Round out the hard edges with a razor blade or small, sharp scissors. Look at the shape from all sides as you work.

be made to look complex by adding separate sculpted details such as fins, wrinkles, teeth, nostrils, etc.

3. **Determining the pattern lines** (Figure 7-7). When the sculpt is complete, draw the center dividing line and the rest of the pattern pieces. As with additive patterning when dividing the skin into pattern pieces, start with the top or the crown and work down. *Note*: it is important to add clear notations and notches to indicate how the pattern pieces fit together before cutting the skin away from the positive.

4. **Removing the skin.** When the pattern lines have been determined, it is time to remove half of the outer surface layer.

Using a sharp razor blade make a 1/8-inch deep incision down the entire center dividing line (Figure 7-8).

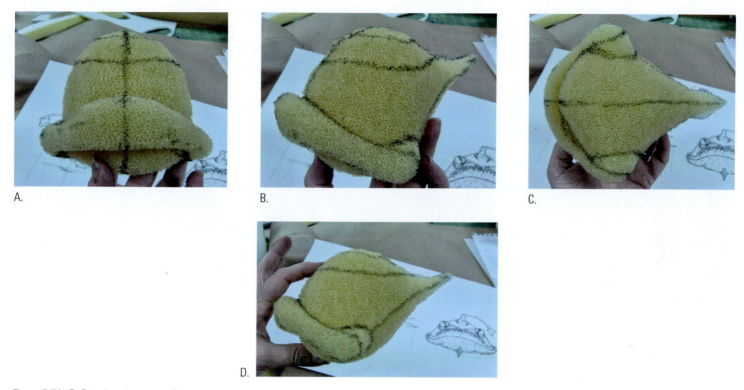

A.

B.

C.

D.

Figure 7-7A–D: Drawing the pattern lines.

Figure 7-8: An entire half of the surface layer can be removed in one go or by the individual piece. The thickness of the surface layer will be approximately 1/8 inch–3/16 inch.

Then carefully pull back the surface layer and slice it off (Figure 7-9).

5. **Cutting apart pattern pieces.** As with additive patterning, the individual pieces need to be cut apart and labeled clearly to indicate placement (Figure 7-10).

A.

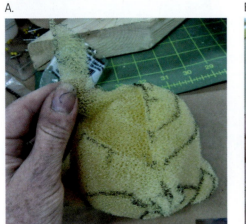

B.

C.

Figure 7-9A–C: Cutting off the rest of the skin.

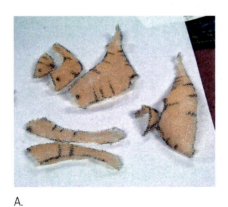

A.

B.

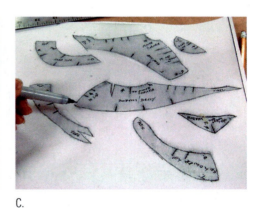

C.

Figure 7-10:
A. Laying out the lamp fish pattern pieces for scaling.
B. Copy of pattern pieces.
C. Pattern pieces completed after being defined with a ruler and marker.

Further Examples of Subtractive Foam Patterning

A.

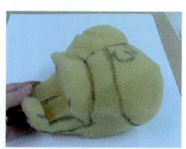

B.

C.

D.

Figure 7-11: Giants for the *Big Friendly Giant*.
A. Designs.
B. Sculpted head.
C. Patterns laid out.
D. Finished head.

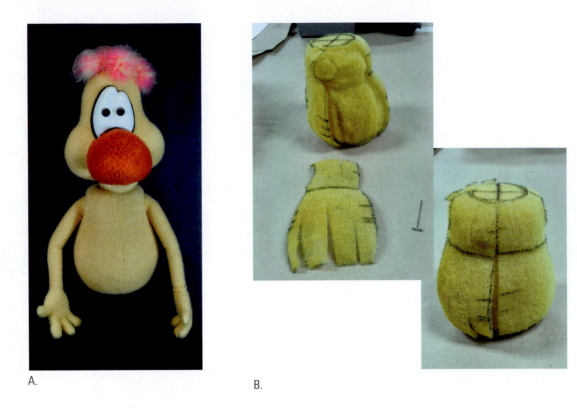

A.

B.

Figure 7-12: Pip.
A. Finished puppet.
B. Body sculpt with half the skin removed.

chapter eight

speed patterning

Speed Patterning

Three minutes later...

Patterning Complete

1. If the pattern is for an object, whether it is worn as with armor, or not worn, as with a prop, it will still probably need to be scaled to the desired size.
2. Before jumping into the foam assembly, even the experienced craftsperson will probably need to construct a mock-up out of less expensive polyether upholstery foam. This step will help solve the challenge of where to bevel edges to get the appropriate angles and contours.

For armor *closed-cell foam* would be the suggested material to use. Many foam crafters use the interconnecting, closed-cell anti-fatigue mats. These can be found at Home Depot, Lowes, Harbor Freight, etc. in the color gray, and in 5/8–inch to 3/4-inch thick sheets (Figure 8-1).

Consideration should be given to how the item will be used. If the item is something that will get a lot of hard use, a foam construction method and finishing technique that is equal to the task should be used.

Speed Patterning

Speed patterning is a term used to describe a process utilizing an existing pattern that has been drafted by hand or on a computer. Just like all clothing patterns the pattern pieces are printed out as flat shapes. The assembly goes very quickly once a pattern has been created. Along the same lines, it would be especially interesting to see Simplicity and Vogue patterns used to build foam clothing.

Speed patterning has primarily been associated with constructing foam armor. There are many examples on the Web and you can find foam interpretations of different armor such as Iron Man and Bobba Fett if you search. Several points should be considered when using prepared patterns:

Figure 8-1: Gray anti-fatigue mat.

Figure 8-2: Samples of patterns that can be used for speed patterning.

Figure 8-3: Scaling the pattern.

Steps in the Speed Patterning Process

1. **Paper pattern.** If the pattern that is being used is a commercial clothing pattern or has been purchased as a "ready-made armor pattern", then there is a good possibility that all the pieces have been trued-up to fit together. It is advisable to build a mock-up to make sure everything has been accounted for. The mock-up will also solve the question of where bevels should be cut. *Note*: because clothing patterns are designed to be used for fabric, seam allowances are generally included. If attempting to build a foam piece with clothing patterns, cut away the seam allowances.

2. **Scale to desired size** (Figure 8-3). If a mock-up is built then you will be able to tell if the size is appropriate. The pattern can also be sketched out on a life-sized mannequin.

3. **Transfer to foam.** Lay out the pattern pieces and transfer them neatly with a fine point marker. The pattern pieces should then be flipped and traced to build the opposite side.

Tip

If you are using a commercial pattern or one that has been pre-made for you, then chances are that the notches and notes labeling each pattern piece are in place. If you are making your own patterns, time should be taken to add as many notations as possible to the pieces. See *Chapter 10*.

4. **Cut out shapes.** Using the appropriate cutting tool cut out all the shapes. Those needing beveling should be left with a small seam allowance so that they can be cut as the object is being to put together (Figure 8-4).

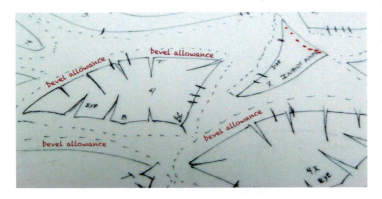

Figure 8-4: Bevel allowance added to foam pieces.

5. **Bevel edges as you put them together.** It is best to glue and assemble the object in a deliberate direction. For example, start from a point such as the nose or the crown of the head and build out from there. See *Chapter 15.*

Taking Patterns from Existing Objects

Occasionally it is possible to discover interesting shapes in the form of ornaments and curios that could be used as foundation shapes for designs. Organic and/or geometric shapes can be utilized for their patterned shape, then reinterpreted or modified for use with foam.

Rigid Curios and Toys

Rigid objects such as curios made from ceramic, plastic, or metal can easily have a skin applied. The skin can be rubber or plastic and tape. As with the additive and subtractive methods, after the skin has been applied, the shapes can be divided with pattern lines, cut apart, and laid out on paper.

A.

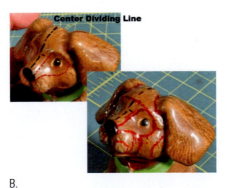

B.

C.

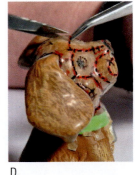

D.

Figure 8-5: Ceramic dog figurine.

A. Cover with the chosen skin material. For the ceramic dog four layers of balloon latex were added by dipping.

B. When the latex has dried, add a center dividing line with marker and follow through with pattern shapes sketched in red. (Because the ears were left out of this part of the process, some of the pattern edges on the side of the head were estimated.)

C. When all the parts have been drawn in red, confirm and go over all the lines with a black felt tip marker.

D. Cut half the shape off down the center line.

E. Half of the skin removed.

F. Cut the pattern pieces apart and tape down.

G. For the mock-up, the patterns were blown up 400 percent on a copy machine. (Because some of the pattern lines were estimated due to the ears, it was very important to put together a loose mock-up.)

H. Finished loose mock-up of ceramic dog. Lines indicate reshaping pieces, adding darts, bevels, and notches. Mock up nose to help determine finished look.

I. Reticulated foam head with a bulbous nose and small mock ear. Mouth plate has been installed.

J. Finished foam head with carved details and mock-up ear.

Soft Sculpted Animals or Stuffed Animals

Any stuffed animal and the resulting parts, when dissected carefully and beveled correctly, can be used for foam construction.

A.

B.

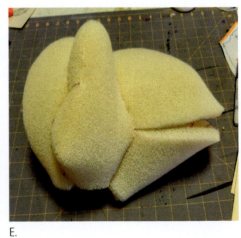

C.

D.

E.

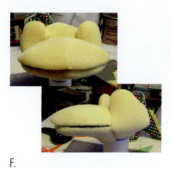

F. G. H. I.

Figure 8-6: Spotted T-Rex toy.

A. Add a center dividing line with chalk, pins, or string.
B. Cut half of the shape away or use the whole fabric object for a pattern. The fabric skin becomes the pattern pieces.
C. Flatten out the pattern pieces by separating the darts and seams. Cut away all seam allowances. If the pieces still do not lie flat then add strategic darts.
D. Copy the flattened fabric pattern pieces to make a paper copy for notes and scaling purposes.
E. Head with no mouth plate.
F. First finished foam T-Rex with *wide* mouth plate.
G. Second finished head with *narrow* mouth plate. Head is getting a bit more *volume* because it is stretched less by the mouth plate.
H. Third finished head with a narrower mouth plate. This, with the addition of a wedge at center, gives more bulge to the snout.
I. Front view of the foam wedge inserted into upper snout. (Always make a mock-up before committing to the real thing.)

chapter nine

free-form foam patterning

Figure 9-1: Cutting a rectangle.

Free-form foam construction involves bending and cutting pieces of foam to achieve the desired form. This can be a fun way to familiarize yourself with foam. My very first experience with foam was with the free-form technique and I recommend this for anyone who is just beginning. See *Chapter 21* using this construction method for the "blue rhino".

Here's an illustrated step–by–step method for a puppet head:

1. Cut out a rectangle (suggested size: 18 inches by 12 inches) (Figure 9-1).
2. Glue the long sides together. Now you have a cylinder (Figure 9-2).
3. On one end make a series of pie-wedge cuts called *darts* (Figure 9-3).

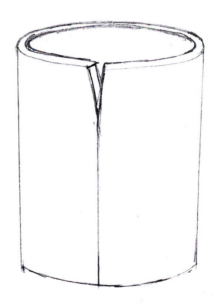

Figure 9-2: Making a cylinder.

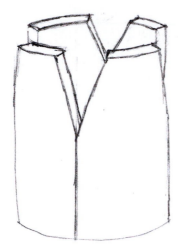

Figure 9-3: Pie-wedge cuts or darts with blunt ends.

Figure 9-4: Darts closed. Notice the blunt, unclosed end.

4. Glue all sides of the blunt darts together. Because of the type of dart being used, this end will round out but not close (Figure 9-4). This end could be the crown of a head, one *side* of a head, a cheek, or a chin (Figure 9-5).

5. Now dart and shape the other end. This set of darts could be fewer in number or shallower, which will make this end a different-looking round shape (Figure 9-6).

6. Glue this set of darts together.

7. Decide what this shape might be. A head, or a bean, or a pumpkin . . .—it could be anything at this point (Figure 9-7). If a mouth is desired then draw a light-colored line to determine the placement. The mouth can be anywhere on this shape (Figure 9-8).

8. An alternate solution is to cut the open end of the cylinder and dart the top and bottom edges. This configuration will turn into a snouted shape (Figure 9-9).

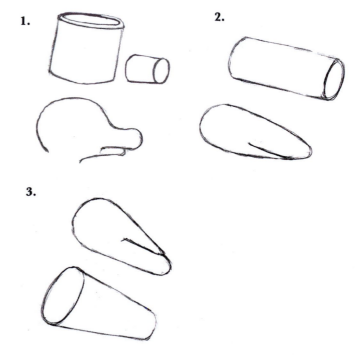

Figure 9-5: Optional shapes this end could be.

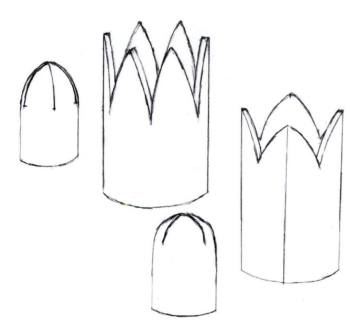

Figure 9-6: The different configurations and depth of darts can produce variations on shape.

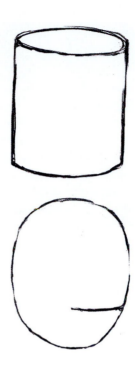

Figure 9-8: Mouth placement.

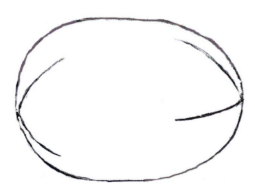

Figure 9-7: Cylinder closed on both ends. What could it become?

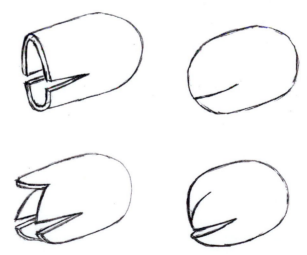

Figure 9-9: Slightly different variation on snout and mouth placement.

Tip

A good rule of thumb about mouth placement: try to cut a mouth opening that is straight across and not curved (Figure 9-10). To accommodate a curved mouth the mouth plate will need to be set at a tight angle and could cause the wrist to be bent in an awkward position. A "mouth plate" is a term used to describe the palette inserted into the puppet's mouth. This can be made of a soft or rigid material.

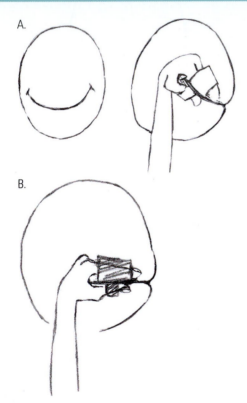

A.

B.

Figure 9-10: Mouth angle.

A. Awkward mouth angle.

B. Angle of mouth more comfortable on wrist.

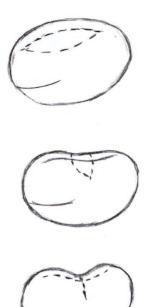

Figure 9-11: Altering the shape.

9. After the position of the mouth has been determined, pinch, stitch, dart, carve, and/or add additional pieces of foam to get the desired shape (Figure 9-11).

10. When the mouth plate has been installed, the finished shape can be painted or covered with fabric such as antron fleece or spandex.

11. The *finishing process,* which includes detail work such as painting, adding features (eyes, hair, teeth, texture, and clothing), should never be rushed. The "details" can breathe life into whatever you are creating or ruin the final result. See *Chapter 20*. I have seen many puppets and other foam objects that have a wonderful foundation shape but the finishing steps were rushed or done poorly so the end result was disappointing. Budget time for all the steps in the process and the finished product will look great!

SECTION IV

DETERMINING THE PATTERN DIVISIONS, "TRUING" PATTERNS, AND CHANGING SCALE

chapter ten

determining the pattern divisions

This chapter will explain the methodology behind determining pattern lines. After the positive is finished, and the outer surface layer has been determined, the next step is to determine *where* the pattern lines (creating each pattern piece) should be drawn.

Anyone who creates patterns knows that the same sculptural shape can be altered by a variation in the placement, number, and complexity of pattern pieces. The only way to gain that patterning experience and knowledge comes from a willingness to take the time to experiment and play with ways to achieve different shapes.

Figure 10-1: An object that is symmetrical.

Steps Towards Determining the Pattern Lines

Before drawing the pattern lines, decide if you want to make an object that is symmetrically patterned (Figure 10-1 is the mirror image of the opposite side), or if your object is asymmetrical (Figure 10-2 is different from the opposite side).

After the skin has been applied to the positive sculpt with the *additive method* (see *Chapter 6*) or the skin has been cut away from the positive sculpt with the subtractive method

Figure 10-2: An object that is asymmetrical.

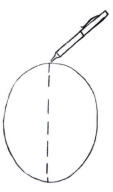

Figure 10-3: Center dividing line.

Figure 10-4: Using the uncut side as a construction guide for the mock-up and final foam piece.

(see *Chapter 7*), a *center dividing line* is drawn to delineate both sides (Figure 10-3) and is a good place to start making a pattern. There are two reasons for this step:

1. This is a standard step towards making a set of patterns for a symmetrical shape. There may be a slight differentiation between the two sides of your positive sculpt side, so you can choose the side you prefer and mirror it.
2. When assembling the final foam pieces into the desired shape, the "uncut" side of the skin still sitting on the positive sculpt can be used as a guide to help determine where the pieces fit (Figure 10.4). *Note*: you should add copious labels and notches to indicate where and how the pieces fit together. The addition of a three-dimensional sample helps a great deal.

The pattern pieces are then drawn onto the rest of the positive. When dividing the skin into pattern pieces, start with the top or the crown and work down (Figure 10-5).

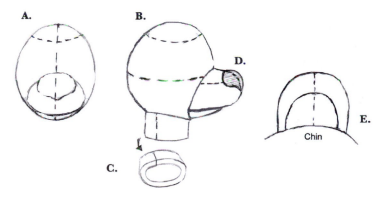

Figure 10-5: Head with muzzle.
A. Crown of object.
B. Side of object.
C. Neck.
D. Muzzle.
E. Chin/mouth.

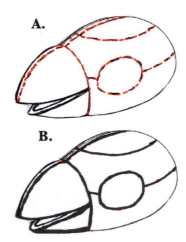

Figure 10-6: Drawing shapes.

A. Drawn with red or blue marker.

B. Finalized with a black marker.

When drawing, keep lines and shapes round and fluid. Continue and draw the same lines onto both sides. When the bigger part of the shape has been divided into sections, move to the smaller areas.

When determining and drawing pattern lines, use two different colored markers. Draw the initial lines with a red or blue sharpie and when you are satisfied with the layout, go over these with a black sharpie. Alcohol, which is usually a good solvent for sharpies, does not work on rubber skin coverings, therefore any colored lines that have been drawn incorrectly can be drawn over or corrected with the second black line.

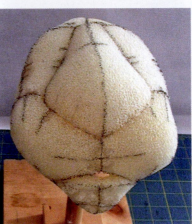

Figure 10-7: Foam "Tiger A" (top) and "Tiger B" (bottom). The same shape altered with two different pattern configurations. "Tiger B" depicts the younger, less developed shape.

Pattern Divisions and Orientation

As mentioned previously there are many ways to "plump up" or "streamline" a foam shape just by subtracting or adding to the amount of pattern pieces and their shapes.

Before drawing pattern lines, consideration should be given to how any shapes such as noses, cheeks, ears, and eye ridges on the positive will be included in the larger shape (see *Chapter 5*). For example the tiger head includes a protuberant nose and ears. If these are cut away and left until a later stage then the larger head and snout area can be patterned more cleanly (Figure 10-8).

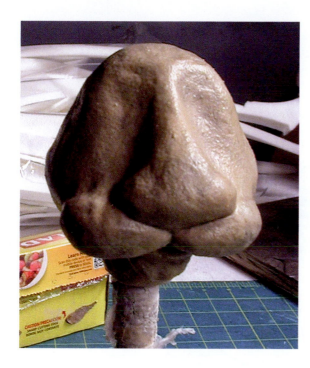

Figure 10-8: Tiger head positive without ears and without separate bulbous nose.

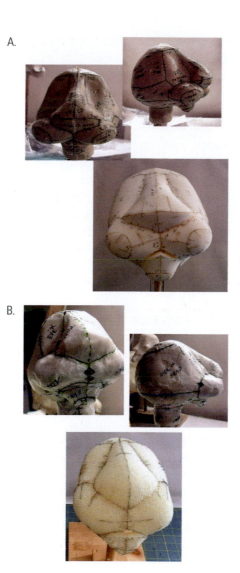

In terms of pattern layout, appropriate patterning can make a big difference to how protuberant a shape can be. Practice and experience will help make this process more understandable and fluid. "Tiger A's" more prominent and bulbous cheeks are produced by adding a round piece at the center of the cheek (Figure 10-9A). This is because under force the foam is buckling and bulging out. Furthermore, the action of bending a whole piece of foam will in fact compress it slightly.

The less bulbous cheek of "Tiger B" is produced by merely bending a whole piece of foam and cupping it with darts. Bending foam at an increasingly tighter angle causes the tiny air cells to become slightly compressed. Darts can help release the tension. Notice too that "Tiger B's" cheek has fewer pieces and the shape was simplified (Figure 10-9B).

Figure 10-9. "Tiger A" and "Tiger B"—notice the nose and cheek area. The addition of the mouth plate will flatten out the cheeks.

A. "Tiger A" clay sculpt with latex skin applied. Finished foam below.

B. "Tiger B" clay sculpt with plastic wrap and tape skin applied. Finished foam below.

Understanding the correct placement of darts and how to bevel foam edges is equally as important as knowing the number of pattern pieces. When looking at a shape and deciding where to add pattern lines, let the object inform the process.

1. Any areas that are large, flat, surface planes, which curve to form big shapes, can be divided up in different ways depending on how big the final product will be. It is not critical to the *shape* to break these patterns up into pieces. The exception to this is if the pattern piece is too big to be placed on the copy machine or if the same pattern may need to be divided into several sections to fit on the raw foam sheets, i.e. the small puppet head can be left as the full pattern piece, whereas a larger scale puppet head with big pieces may need to be cut down to more manageable sizes.
2. If the there is a sharp angle or contour anywhere on the shape, then there should be a pattern break or a series of breaks to allow the foam to make the turn (Figure 10-10).
3. If the *edges* of the pattern pieces need to "cup" or make a partial hemisphere, then you will need to use darts (Figure 10-11). The necessity to add darts will become obvious during the "transfer of the pattern skin to paper process" mentioned in *Chapter 11*.

After the correct pattern shapes have been cut, the experienced patternmaker knows where to add dividing lines, darts, and bevels to get the desired shape. Again, practice is the way to really get a feel for this process. Beveling and darting is further discussed in *Chapter 15*.

Adding Notes, Labels, and Notches

The importance of proper labeling has been mentioned several times in previous chapters. The reason being that on an original shape, when the pieces are cut away and flattened out, chances are that it will be almost impossible to discern what they are and where they fit. When labeling pattern pieces consider adding them after the pattern lines have been drawn and while

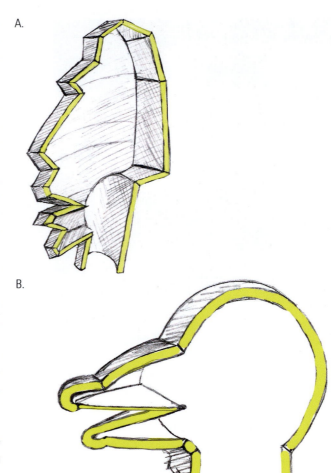

A.

B.

Figure 10-10: Identifying angles and sharp contours.

A. Sharp contours.

B. Sharp and slightly round contours.

Figure 10-11: The cheek pattern from the plastic wrap skin from "Tiger B". Notice the new shape after the darts are added and how the piece lays flat.

the pieces are still in place on the positive sculpt. You can use any system you prefer. For example, you could use numbers or letters. I prefer to use a combination of notches, notes, and abbreviations.

- *Notches* are small symbols or slashes drawn on the edges of patterns to indicate how and where the pieces fit together.
- Abbreviations such as "CF" (center front), "CB" (center back), "T" (top), and "B" (bottom) are very helpful for determining orientation.
- *Labels* or notations such as "head side", "muzzle side", or "neck" are all helpful but if the initial pattern skin is very small then these will be difficult to add.

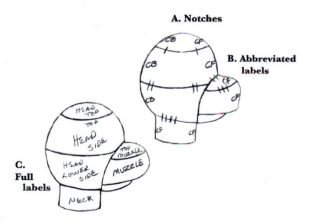

A. Notches

B. Abbreviated labels

C. Full labels

Figure 10-12: Labeling patterns still on the positive sculpt.

A. Adding notches to patterns.

B. Example of CF and CB.

C. Labels such as "head side" and "neck" can also be added to help with deciphering the pieces.

When Patterning Goes Wrong

chapter eleven

transferring patterns
to paper and "truing"
pattern pieces

Transferring Patterns to Paper

Whether you used *plastic and tape*, *fabric*, *rubber* or decided to use the skin intrinsic to the positive sculpt (see *Chapter 7*), notice that some if not all the pieces do not want to lie flat. It is crucial that each piece lies flat so that they can be transferred to a flat sheet of foam. The curved or "cupped" aspect of the skin is what is needed to help determine dart placement and care should be taken when flattening the pieces that the clues to where to "slash and spread" the patterns are not lost.

"Slash and spread" is a patterning term pertaining to splitting a clothing pattern into several sections to expand the size or shape. In this instance it simply means *slashing* into the cupped shape and as the slash *spreads* open, the more the shape flattens out.

With a blade or scissors, make a small slash at approximately a right angle to the side and then gently depress the pattern piece with your finger. Notice that as the piece spreads open forming a "V" the pattern piece begins to flatten

By this point, the dividing lines of the pattern pieces have been drawn and the notes and notches needed to differentiate each piece have been added. Half of the "pattern skin" has also been removed from the positive.

A.   B.   C.

Figure 11-1: To get the cupped pieces to lie flat, small incisions called *darts* must be cut to allow the arcs to spread open.

A. Start with a curved piece. Cut the cupped piece to spread it open.

B. Many incisions may be needed to get the piece to lie flat.

C. Paper pattern split to increase curvature,

out. If the pattern piece is still cupping, carefully make more incisions and between each cut, then gently depress the piece to see if it can completely flatten out. You may decide that it is better at this point to cut a pattern piece completely apart, making several smaller pieces, in order to flatten them out. This is okay; however, careful notation on each piece should be made as they are being separated or you most definitely will forget where and how they go together.

When the pieces are able to flatten out, it is time to lay them out on paper. *Note*: never stretch or mash the pattern skin pieces to flatten them. This will crush the curves indicated by the pattern skin and cause the eventual foam shape to be malformed.

Tip

When using the "slash and spread" method, the incisions turn into darts. When working with fabric the pinched tucks or "darts" used to contour fabric to the positive shape will open up to create a triangle-shaped void (Figure 11-2).

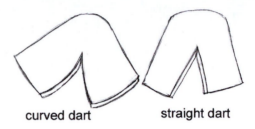

curved dart   straight dart

Figure 11-2 The dart.

Tip

The majority of darts should be cut at approximately a *right* angle to the edge of the pattern piece (Figure 11-3).

*Cut at approximately 90 degrees

Figure 11-3: Try to cut darts at a right angle.

The Pattern Whisperer

When all the pieces are flattened out with a little pressure, it is time to tape each piece to paper. Place each piece on the paper and carefully depress each side again and tape it as you go. Be careful that the thinner areas of pattern skin do not buckle. Depending on the color of your "skin" material, you may want to choose a paper that contrasts with the pattern piece (Figure 11-4).

Tip

An alternative to taping the pieces to paper is laying the pieces directly on the copy machine screen and letting the lid depress the pieces flat.

Tip

If you have pattern pieces pertaining to a nose, an ear, or separate features, it is helpful (and also a little amusing) to segregate those pattern pieces to individual sheets of paper, e.g. a sheet of nose parts, a sheet of ear parts, a sheet of hand parts, etc.

When the pattern skins are all taped down, make a copy of each sheet. If the pieces are very small, you can enlarge them to make them easier to see. Make notes on how much you enlarged them for the scaling process still to come.

Truing Pattern Pieces

After the paper copy of the skin pieces has been made, you can "true-up" your patterns. "Truing" means correcting any major discrepancies drawn onto the pattern, e.g. straightening wiggly lines, aligning sides that are not even, correcting curves that are irregular, etc. I always use a combination of rulers (both curved and straight) but, if you are careful, *free-hand correction*

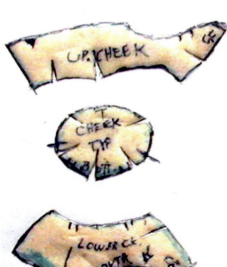

Figure 11-4: Taping the pattern skin to paper.

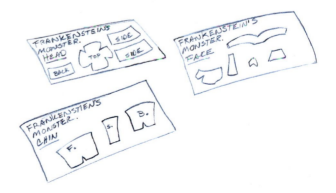

Figure 11-5

A.

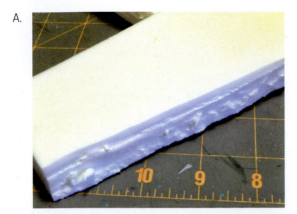

B.

Figure 11-6:
A. Badly cut foam.
B. Joining two badly cut pieces together.

(not using a ruler) can also work. Remember the line at the edge of the pattern is the cut edge of each foam piece. It is important that these edges are as smooth as possible (Figure 11-6). If the edge is roughly cut or cut at an odd angle then it can affect the way the pieces join together and distort the overall shape.

Trace around the edges of each pattern piece with a ruler and pencil to even out wiggly lines and curves (Figure 11.8).

When the refinement of lines is complete, then cut out the individual pattern shapes. Most of the pieces can be placed

Figure 11-7: Photo of different rulers or guides that can be used to help with curves.

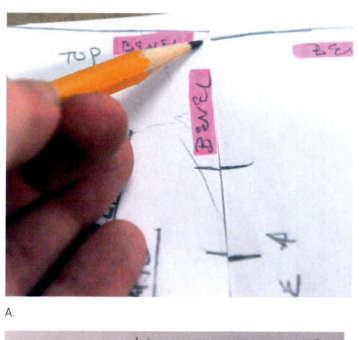

A.

B.

C.

D.

Figure 11-8: Demonstrating truing-up.

A. Trimming pattern sides to make them even.

B. Smoothing out curves without compromising the pattern.

C. A curve that is too distorted.

D. After cutting out each piece, make certain the notches line up.

side by side to check if the notches are aligning correctly and to see if the sides match each other.

- If the sides of the patterns do not align, then tape a small scrap of paper to the edge and redraw the line. Tape the backside of the pattern where it overlaps also to make sure that the "pattern patch" will stay on.
- If the notches do not match use paint or draw over the mismatching notches and redraw them when the patterns are side by side. Again notches are a huge help when gluing foam pieces together, especially if the pieces are under tension and need to be encouraged with a little force to fit together.

This is also a good time to add any additional pertinent notes or labels that can help differentiate the pieces. I often include notes or symbols indicating where beveling will need to occur. On these areas of the pattern, you can use arrows or any notes that will help you remember. As the final foam pieces are being cut out, these additional notes will help indicate where a foam *seam allowance* or *bevel allowance* might need to be added.

Tip

After the "scaling process" has occurred and before the final foam is cut, I often highlight (with a bright color) the paper patterns to add additional focus to edges that will need a bevel. This will remind me to add the bevel allowance when tracing and cutting the foam pieces (Figure 11-9).

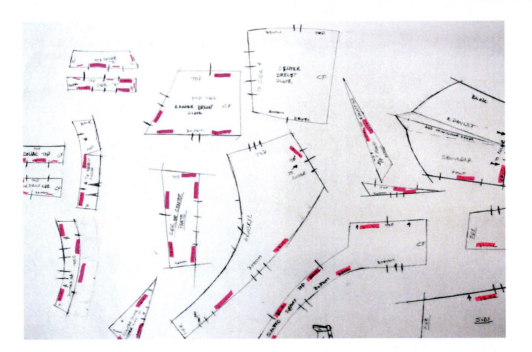

Figure 11-9: Highlighting the paper patterns.

chapter twelve

scale: determining the size of the finished piece

Figure 12-1: The overhead projector.

The term *scale* or *scaling* means to increase or reduce the size of a pattern or shape. The goal of this step is to determine how big you want the finished piece to be and, therefore, how many times you will need to multiply the sculpted positive to reach the desired size.

It is sometimes possible to make the positive sculpt the same size as the finished piece. Therefore no scaling of the pattern is necessary because the pattern pieces you cut off the sculpt will be the actual size of the real pattern pieces. However, when patterning big items such as costume characters, big props, scenic pieces, and large puppets, it is often more convenient to sculpt a smaller scale of the original.

Determining Size with an Overhead Projector

One way to determine the size of the finished object is by using a technique utilized by scenic artists and mural painters. The *overhead projector* has been used for years to project and enlarge small designs onto large, two-dimensional surfaces (Figure 12-1). This same technique can be used for scaling by enlarging a two-dimensional design and projecting it onto a three-dimensional object.

To use an overhead projector you will first need to transfer the design to acetate. Insert the acetate into a copy machine's paper feed tray and then it is possible to reproduce the design. If a copy machine is not available, it is also possible to hand trace the design onto acetate (Figure 12-2).

Cover the wall with paper where you intend to project the image. Tape or pin it so that it is stable. If you are lucky enough to have a live model, ask them to stand in front of the paper and trace their rough outline with a red or blue marker. You can also use a mannequin or dress form (Figure 12-3).

Project the acetate copy of the two-dimensional design onto the model standing in front of the paper. Move the projector forward and backward while adjusting the focus to

Figure 12-2: Transfer design to acetate.

approximate the finished size. With this tool you can see how big the head and body of the character will be in relation to the human form.

The other advantage of this method is that you can see where the design allows for sightline possibilities or "vision ports" (when building an object that will be worn) and where the design might need to be tweaked to adjust proportions such as if the head, feet, or hands are just too big (Figure 12-4). It is possible to make adjustments for the head, and the rest of the individual parts of the body with this method. You may end up with a silhouette that has a 20 percent smaller head, a 10 percent larger body, and 15 percent smaller hands. All the proportions can be tweaked and still maintain the overall feel of the design. When all the size adjustments and modifications are completed and traced, you can then go back and trace details such as the nose, eyes, teeth, and eyebrows as needed.

A.

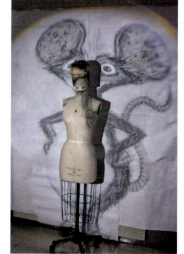

B.

Figure 12-3:
A. Project onto a mannequin or live model.
B. Mouse character projected onto form.

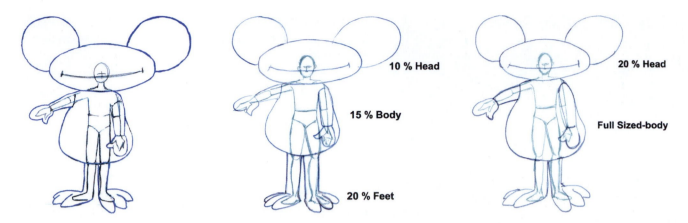

Figure 12-4A–C: Modifying individual proportions to fit a model.

When the image has been adjusted to the desired size, trace the outline of the design with a black marker over the top of the model's red or blue outline. Remember the goal of this process is to determine how big or small the finished design will be. Start out by getting the proportions correct, and then fill in the details of the features after the big shapes are determined (Figure 12-5).

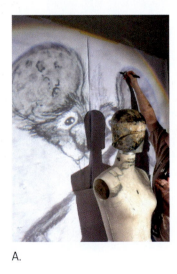

A.

B.

Figure 12-5:
A. Tracing the projection.
B. Filling in details.

Proportion Considerations When Scaling a Costume Character or Worn Object

1. Keep in mind that if the character has arms, a wide body, and is life size, a big part of the "body" of the object will absorb the length of the human arm (Figure 12-6). Unless the costume has arm extensions the practical arm will be very short. Consider whether the character needs a high level of hand articulation or if the arms only need to flap. It is possible to add articulated extensions to arms if necessary, but you want to have that in the plan before you start construction.

    The same principal applies to human legs. If the character or object's crotch hangs to the knee area on the human actor, then this could limit movement unless a plan has been put in place. This could involve the actor incorporating the stylized movement into the character or modifying the character's body to allow for more leg dexterity.

2. The number and/or size of fingers for some costume character hands can sometimes cause a lot of friction inhibiting movement. The adult human palm where the fingers join is roughly between 4 inches and 6 inches

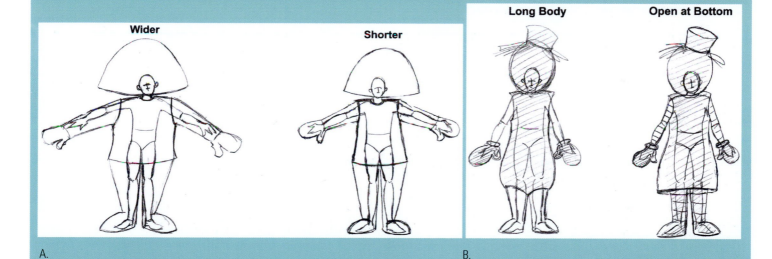

Figure 12-6: Human inside character.

A. A wide body shortens arms, therefore narrowing shoulders can help arms move.

B. A long body on a character costume extending past the human hip joint will shorten the stride of the actor. Opening the bottom of the character and therefore creating a larger area for leg movement, will increase the actor's stride.

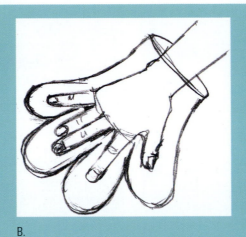

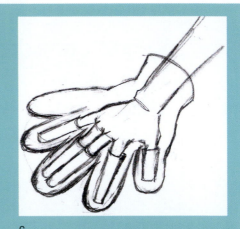

A.

B.

C.

Figure 12-7: Costume character hands.

A. Human hand inside over-sized character hands.

B. Limiting the number of fingers.

C. Extending fingers around palm.

depending on the person. If the fingers on the character are big and expected to correspond with the human hand this can sometimes limit flexibility (Figure 12.7). A good solution is to limit the number of fingers or extend the character fingers further around the palm.

Again mechanical extensions to the arms with moving articulation can be added.

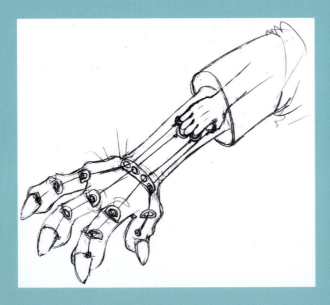

Figure 12-8: Extension inside character arm.

Freehand Sketching to Determine Size

The second method for determining visual scale involves freehand sketching of the final size. If you are making an object, puppet, or anything worn on the body, utilize the same technique as the overhead projector but *freehand sketch* the ideal size. The big sketch does not need to be exact or as detailed as the design. This is only to get a sense of size. Capturing the *mass* (how much space it will take up) of the object is the goal (Figure 12-9).

what will be controlling the puppet is helpful information (Figure 12-10).

A.

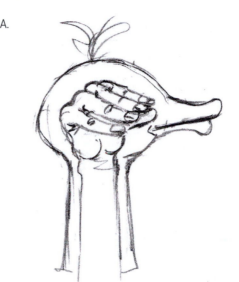

B.

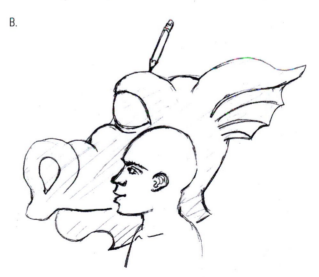

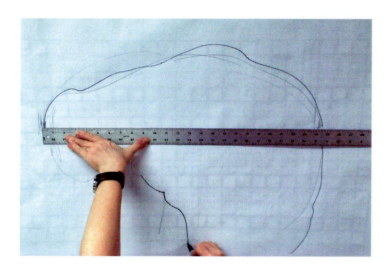

Figure 12-9: With no overhead projector, freehand sketching is a quick and easy way to get a sense of the finished size.

If building a body or hand puppet, hold up the arm and hand to see how big the proportion of the head will be in conjunction with the size of a real hand and length of the forearm. This can also apply to the mouth plate. Puppet mouths can be controlled by small or very large triggers, individual fingers, entire hands, or whole bodies, therefore the size of

Figure 12-10:
A. Freehand sketching over an arm or a hand.
B. Sketching over a model's head.

If building a breastplate or helmet and there is no dress form or mannequin to work from, you can trace the model's outline onto paper and then roughly sketch in how big the details of the armor might be. It is also possible to get a rough idea of the size of some armor, such as a breastplate, by using an actor's measurement sheet.

After going through the process of determining the desired size of the finished object or costume, the next step is to reduce or enlarge your pattern.

chapter thirteen

formula for reducing and enlarging

For *reducing* and *enlarging* it is easy to use the same standard formula used by quilters and other crafters. With the formula given in *Chapter 12*, you can get the approximate size of your design. *Note*: it is recommended after reducing or enlarging patterns, to first build a mock-up with the newly scaled pieces before continuing with the final foam assembly. The mock-up will:

1. Tell you if the overall shape is satisfactory and if you need to modify the pattern shapes or the beveling.
2. Tell you if you need to enlarge or reduce the pattern.

A Visual of What the Formula is Doing

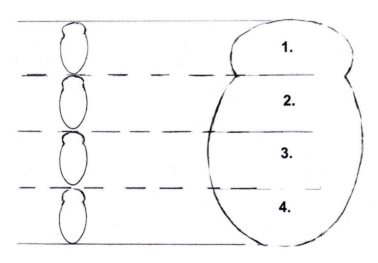

Figure 13-1: Smaller positive sculpt and desired size of the finished piece.

How and What to Measure to Plug into the Formula

1. **Measuring the positive sculpt.** Take a measurement of the width and height of the positive sculpt. If the positive sculpt

is small enough, the handiest tool to use is a set of calipers. Tighten the wingnut on the calipers to lock the arms and the measurement, and then lay the spread arms on a ruler (Figure 13.2).

A.

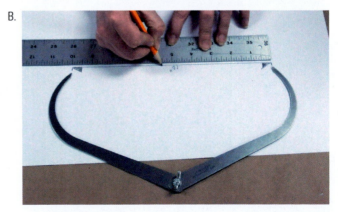

B.

Figure 13-2: Positive sculpt measured with calipers.
A. Length was the most significant measurement for this piece.
B. Getting measurements from calipers.

2. **Measuring the finished piece.** Using a yardstick, tape measure, or T-square, take the same measurements (width and length) using the enlargement made with the overhead projector or the freehand-scaled sketch from Chapter 12. *Note*: only one of these measurements will need to be plugged into the formula. However, taking the two different measurements will give you a choice of the most important measurement. Because of the prep work on the designs and working drawings done during the design phase, the profile views should be ready to help when determining the finished size.

If enlarging something that is narrow in width, long, and tall in height, which measurement should dictate the enlargement or reduction? A student sculpted a horse positive and decided to use the profile or side height/length. When the puppet was enlarged and built, the front width was a bit narrower than desired. Pick the *width measurement* or *height measurement* that works for you by measuring the scaled drawing. Consider how the item will be used. Will it be a puppet controlled by a human hand or a costume character whose size is dictated by how the arms coordinate with the actor's arms? These are the factors to consider when choosing which side to take the measurements for scaling.

Figure 13-3: Make your own slide ruler. Measure length of finished piece with a T-square and a yardstick.

Note: make certain that the measurement you choose is the same view from both sides, i.e. front width of positive sculpt and front width of scaled finished piece. A "profile" measurement from one and a "front" measurement from the other will foul up the final product.

After deciding which set of measurements best fits the needs of the design, the next step is plugging the measurements into the formula.

The Formula

The measurements you will need to plug into the formula:

1. The size of the positive sculpt (PS).
2. The size of the finished piece (FP).

$$FP \div PS = \textit{times enlarged} \ (TE)$$

TE is how many times the PS will need to be multiplied to achieve the size of the FP.

If FP ÷ PS = TE,
then TE x PS = FP.

Enlarging

Example 1
If the PS is 4 inches tall and the FP needs to be 7 inches then:

FP ÷ PS = TE
7 ÷ 4 = 1.75

and

1.75 x 4 = 7.

Solution: patterns made from the 4-inch PS will need to be multiplied 1.75 times to achieve the height of 7 inches.

Type 175 on the copy machine keypad. Copy machines will vary but this will get you close to the desired size.

Example 2

If the FP needs to be 6 feet tall (72 inches) and the PS is 4 inches then:

72 inches ÷ 4 inches = 18

Solution: patterns made from the 4-inch PS will need to be multiplied 18 times to achieve the height of 6 feet.

Type 1800 on the copy machine keypad. Copy machines will vary but this will get you close to the desired size.

Reducing

It is possible to find an existing shape and reduce it to smaller sizes. Use the steps for enlarging in reverse.

Example

If the PS or existing pattern is 6 inches and the finished piece needs to be 2.5 inches, then:

FP ÷ PS = *times reduced* (TR)
FP ÷ PS = TR
2.5 ÷ 6 = 0.416 or 0.42
0.416 x 6 = 2.49 or 2.5

Solution: patterns made using a 6-inch PS will need to be multiplied by 0.42 to get a finished piece that is 2.5 inches tall.

Type 42 on the copy machine keypad. Copy machines will vary but this will get you close to the desired size.

See *Chapter 14* to see how to apply these calculations using a copy machine and a scale grid to produce enlarged or reduced patterns.

chapter fourteen

how to enlarge and reduce pattern pieces

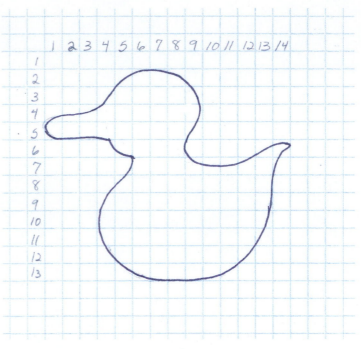

Figure 14-1: Pattern transferred onto grid paper.

There are many methods used by foam artisans when scaling a pattern. The three methods that will be discussed in this chapter are the *grid*, the *copy machine*, and the *experienced eye*.

Of the three, the grid and copy machine methods are the most accurate to use. However, with experience and a practiced eye, the foam artisan can achieve the approximate size more quickly by cutting out the need for scaling.

The Grid Method

The grid method takes a bit of time to achieve but if there is no copy machine available, then it is a good method to know. Mural painters and scenic artists have used the grid method for years. It entails laying a small grid over the item to be transferred, then laying out a larger grid to the desired scale, and plotting out the corresponding points of the image. The points are then connected to transfer the whole image to the larger grid area. For foam patterning it means laying a grid over (or drawing a grid on top of) a pattern taken from the *positive sculpt*. If this is a small pattern, use a 1/4-inch or 1/8-inch grid size. You can hand draw the grid lines or use a copy machine to transfer the pieces to grid paper.

Tip

Two ways to copy onto grid paper:

1. Copy the grid onto a piece of acetate, then tape it on top of your flattened pattern pieces exactly where you want it to line up. When copying them together, the grid overlay shows up on the copy of the pattern sheet.
2. Place grid paper into the copy machine paper feed and duplicate the paper patterns directly on to the grid paper. This will not allow exact control of grid placement.

You need to decide how much you want to enlarge the pattern (see *Chapter 12*). Use the grid as a visual tool for plotting out points. The basic idea is if the pattern needs to be larger use a smaller grid then transfer it to a larger grid.

How to Determine the Larger Grid Size

Note: this calculation is based on the *size of the positive sculpt* and the *size of the finished piece*.

Example 1

Your PS is 3 inches tall and the FP needs to be 9 inches tall (Figure 14-2).

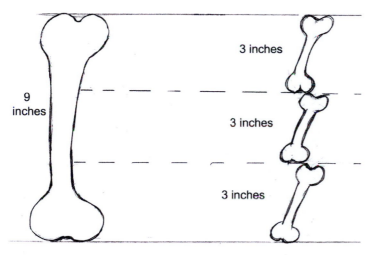

9 inches

3 inches

3 inches

3 inches

Figure 14-2: Positive sculpt and finished piece being measured.

1. $9 \div 3 = 3$; the pattern is being increased in size by 3 times.

2. $3 \times 100 = 300$. The pattern will therefore be enlarged 300 percent.

Because it is pre-drawn, 1/4-inch grid paper is readily available. Use the 1/4-inch layout to calculate the 300 percent needed for the proper enlargement.

Do not forget to modify the fraction to a decimal; *1/4-inch translates to 0.25*.

3. 0.25×3 (the number of times the pattern should be increased) = 0.75
   Solution: you will need a final 3/4-inch grid layout to achieve the enlargement of 3 times or 300 percent.

Again, the grid used for the positive sculpt patterns can be any size, but the corresponding grid used for enlarging should be calculated by multiplying the times needed for the positive sculpt to be enlarged to match the size of the finished piece.

TE x PS grid = enlarged grid size needed.

How To Determine the Smaller Grid Size

Example

If an 8-inch PS or object needs to be reduced to a 3-inch FP.

You will be plotting the positive sculpt patterns on a 2-inch grid.

$3 \div 8 = 0.375$
$0.375 \times 100 = 37.5\%$ reduced
$0.375 \times 2 = 0.75$.
This translates to a 3/4-inch inch grid.

Solution: the 2-inch grid layout needs to be plotted out on a 3/4-inch grid.

How To Plot Out a Pattern on a Grid for Enlarging

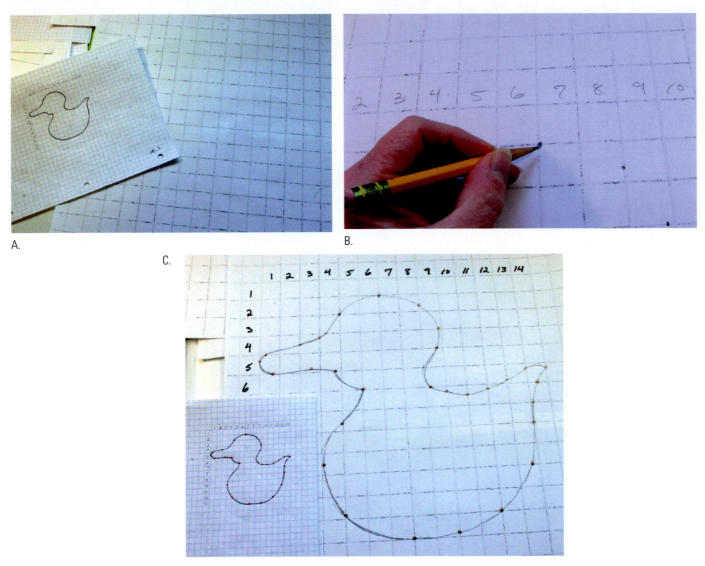

Figure 14-3: Plotting out the points on a grid to expand the patterns.

A. Sample duck on 1/4-inch grid paper.

B. Plotting out the corresponding points.

C. The dots connected.

The Copy Machine Method

To Enlarge the Pattern by Machine

This enlargement method is the faster of the two methods, the downside is that unless you buy your own copy machine, there will be some considerable time spent at the local office supply store *and* a lot of paper can be wasted. *Note*: copy machines and scanners can vary in terms of altering the size of the originals and copies. Always take a ruler and measure the first enlargements or reductions to establish if you need to tweak the number.

On a copy machine everything starts out at 100, which is the baseline. Therefore, to get the appropriate percentage of enlargement needed, multiply by 100.

If a PS is 4 inches tall and the FP needs to be 7 inches then:

7 inches ÷ 4 inches = 1.75
1.75 = times multiplied 1.75 x 100 = 175
175 = percentage of enlargement.

Type 175 on the copy machine keypad. Remember copy machines can vary in accuracy of enlargement and reduction. Always check to make certain the size is the size you need.

If you need to enlarge something to an extremely large size, most copy machines only go to 400 percent (some stores have large scale copiers so use these if they are available!). When using a standard copier to get the desired enlargement you will need to copy the same piece several times to get what you need.

If you have a PS of 4 inches and you want it to be enlarged to a 72-inch FP.

Then 72 ÷ 4 = 18
18 x 100 = 1800
1800 = percentage to be enlarged on a copy machine and it will need to be done in several rounds of copying.

1. 1800% – 400% = 1400% left to enlarge
2. 1400% – 400% = 1000% left to enlarge
3. 1000% – 400% = 600% left to enlarge
4. 600% – 400% = 200% left to enlarge
5. 200% remaining to enlarge.

These would be monstrous pattern pieces. But the copy screen is a limited size, therefore extremely large pattern pieces would need multiple copies to be made and taped together to get the full pattern.

Tip

If needing extremely large patterns: try to find copy stores that have large copy machines for maps and blueprints. The screens are bigger and these can print giant sheets. This will reduce the cutting and taping that happens sometimes when the patterns need to be pieced together.

To Reduce the Pattern by Machine

This is the reverse of the enlargement formula.

Note: if you are making a smaller copy of a finished foam object and you want to use the same pattern, treat it as the original positive sculpt and work backwards.

Example

If you have a 4-inch PS, and you want a 2-inch FP.

FP ÷ PS = reduction
2 ÷ 4 = 0.5
0.5 x 100 = 50

Remember 100 is the baseline on the copy machine, so anything below 100 is reduced and anything above is enlarged.

The Experienced Eye Method

A quick word about this technique: after working with foam objects for many years it is possible to learn by "eye-balling" to estimate approximate size. This can happen after working with roughly the same sized positive sculpt over and over again and seeing what percentage of increase and decrease can get the desired size. Anyone can learn this technique. Governments will not topple because the enlargement of a finished piece is 10 or 20 percent off. So experiment and have fun!

SECTION V

PUTTING IT ALL TOGETHER: FROM PATTERN TO OBJECT

chapter fifteen

how to bevel corners
and utilize darts

Foam provides the unique opportunity to build hollow objects from a straight flat sheet of structural material. This chapter is a basic overview of how to achieve the lovely contours and angles that may be integral to a three-dimensional finished piece.

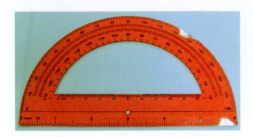

Figure 15-1: Protractor.

A.

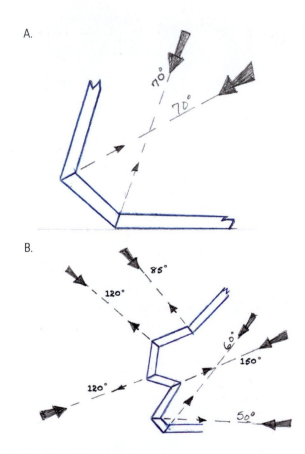

Because it is a dimensional material the edges of foam have a "thickness". When deliberately cutting the edges of foam at angles, it is called "beveling". These are clean, angled cuts that allow for supported, abrupt turns when curved or hard-edged contours are needed. When two beveled edges are put together it is called a *mitered joint.* The term "mitered" is commonly associated with carpentry when installing baseboards, crown molding, and picture frames.

Angles

Using a protractor it is easy to see the angle variation. Two 45-degree cuts on either end of two foam pieces can make a sharp angle, whereas a cut on an angle anywhere between 45 and 90 degrees glued together will create a subtler angle (Figure 15-2).

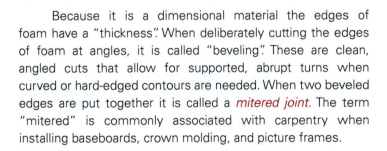

Figure 15-2:
A. 70 degrees.
B. Various degrees.

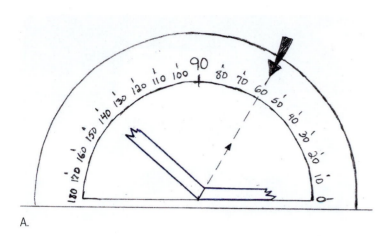

A.

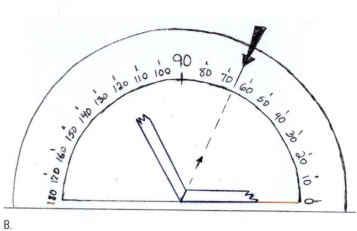

B.

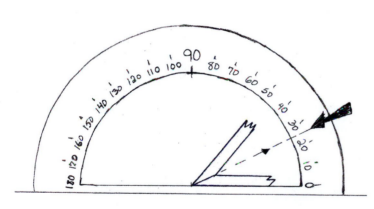

C.

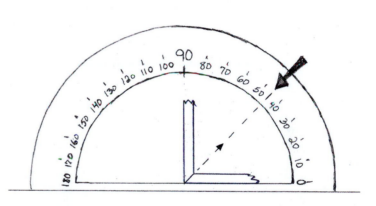

D.

Figure 15-3: Different angles to achieve different shapes.

A. 60 degrees.

B. 65 degrees.

C. 25 degrees.

D. 45 degrees.

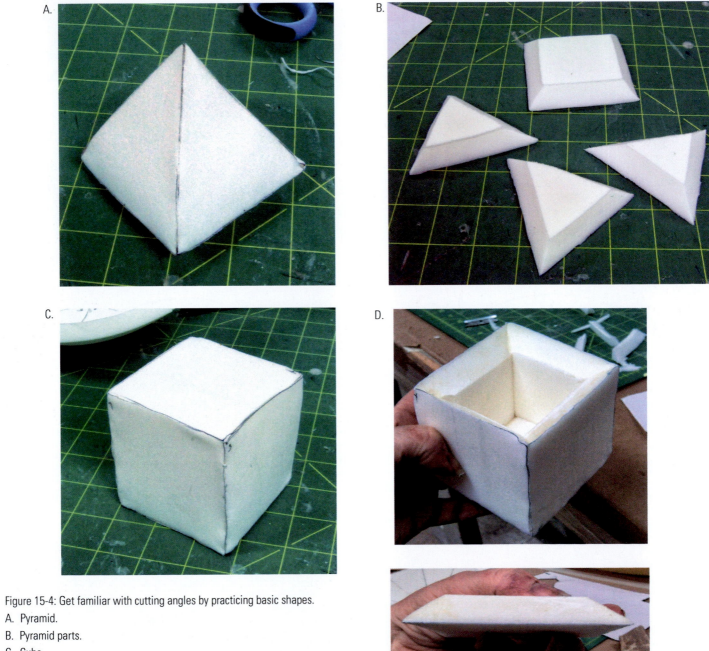

Figure 15-4: Get familiar with cutting angles by practicing basic shapes.

A. Pyramid.

B. Pyramid parts.

C. Cube.

D. Side view of cube part.

Darts and Wedges

As explained in Chapter 11, you can flatten out your positive sculpt skins with careful cutting. The V-shape that is created when the slash opens is called a "dart". Darts are commonly used to contour and curve garments to the body and other objects where fabric is used. By using the same methodology, foam can be made to curve into a bulbous, cupped shape. Experiment with different widths and lengths of darts and you will find you can get a variety of shapes (Figure 15-5).

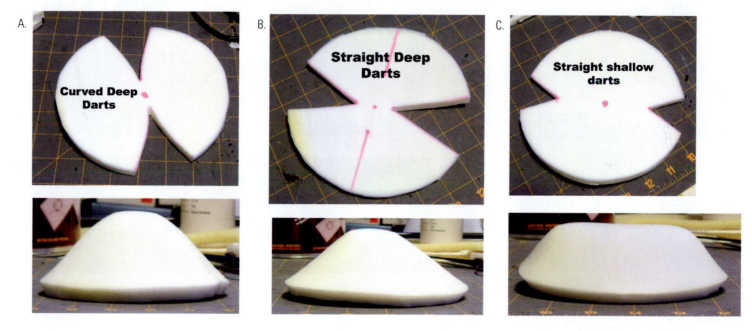

Figure 15-5: Darts.

A. Curved deep.

B. Straight deep.

C. Straight shallow.

One good way to familiarize yourself with the use of darts and wedges is cutting open a beach ball (Figure 15-6). The inflatable beach ball is a thin skin of equal sections put together to form a sphere. Cut the connected wedges open and spread them out to see the darts. Notice that the sections are equal and contoured a certain way.

If the number of sections is increased and the size (width) of each is decreased, the shape becomes more fluid and subtle. If the individual panels become less curved, then the shape becomes narrower and peanut-like. *Note*: none of the panels have beveled edges. To achieve a smooth, round finish when joining multiple panels together, keep the "side cuts" or edges at a precise 90 degrees (Figure 15-7).

Figure 15-6: The six-section beach ball.

A. Half section (with sections connected) of a blue and white beach ball spread on foam and traced.

B. Halves glued together.

C. Multi-colored, six-section beach ball pattern with darts added to center of each wedge to flatten out the slight concavity of the pattern piece.

D. Half of the wedges assembled. Note the addition of the darts to each section eliminated the angular quality of the final shape as seen in Figure 15-6 B.

E. By finessing the shape with a wedge and dart, a peanut-like object can result.

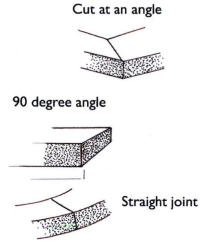

Cut at an angle

90 degree angle

Straight joint

Figure 15-8: The six-section baseball cap.

Figure 15-7: Edges of foam pieces need to be cut at 90 degrees to achieve a smooth round shape.

Baseball caps are like half of a beach ball being a series of "wedge" sections (Figure 15-8).

You can also use a rubber ball. Find the center and divide it into equal sections – as many or as few as desired. If the ball were divided into four sections, the final shape, as with the beach ball, would be a slightly angular sphere. If the sections are big enough to "cup", remember to add darts!

A.

Figure 15-9: Inflatable ball.

A. Divided into eight sections.

B. Cutting out one half section and cutting out of foam.

C. Half of the shape glued together. The more sections a round shape is divided into the more fluid it will become.

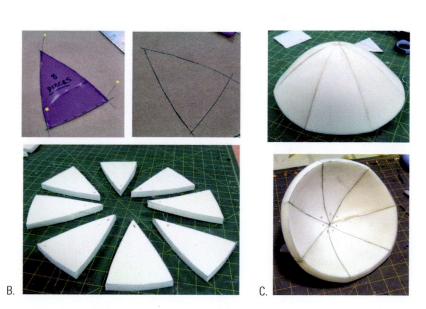

B.

C.

Finding preformed shapes and adapting them can be a handy tool when working with foam (Figure 15-10).

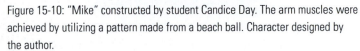

Figure 15-10: "Mike" constructed by student Candice Day. The arm muscles were achieved by utilizing a pattern made from a beach ball. Character designed by the author.

chapter sixteen

cutting pattern pieces out of foam

When the desired size of the pattern pieces has been reached (see *Chapters 12–14*), it is time to cut them out of foam. Again to ensure that you have the correct pattern shapes and that the size is correct, it is suggested that you put together a mock-up out of cheaper, lighter foam such as *polyether urethane upholstery foam*. The pattern shapes and size might need to be altered to get the desired shape. This could save money and time in the long run, if you are using more expensive foam for the finished piece.

When cutting patterns out of foam, spread the entire sheet of foam out on the floor or table and lay out each pattern piece (Figure 16-1). Laying out all the pattern pieces will provide a visual to ensure you have enough foam.

If the pattern is symmetrical, make certain that you leave enough room to double the pattern pieces because you will need to cut one piece for each side (Figure 16-2). Draw a small

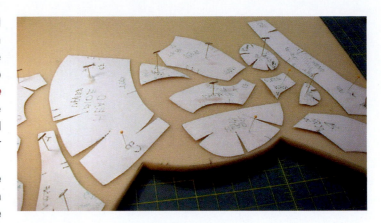

Figure 16-2: Reversing patterns on foam.

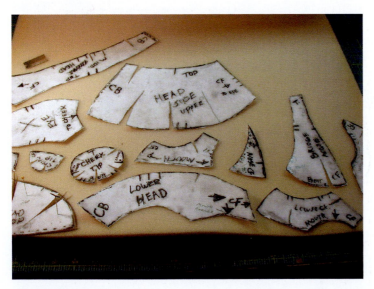

Figure 16-1: Laying out paper pieces.

symbol such as an "x" on the pieces that were traced with the "top side" of the paper pattern up. This will help when dividing the foam parts into piles when beginning the assembly process. It is also a good idea to get familiar with flipping your patterns so that the habit will carry over to fabric and fur cutting (see *Chapter 18*).

You will by this point know which pieces need to be beveled, so allow for some space between those pieces needing extra room. Draw a dotted line or use arrows indicating that extra foam many be needed (Figure 16-3).

When transferring the paper patterns to foam, consider the thickness of the marker being used. *Extra fine point* or *fine point* waterproof markers such as *sharpies* are good for tracing lines around patterns. The size depends on the delicacy and size of the pattern.

If precision is key to the project and there is a fear that the marker lines could show through the finishing fabric, consider cutting the lines off the foam pieces. A marker line that is 1/16 inch thick might add an 1/8 inch to the pattern piece and even more to the finished object when all the patterns are put together

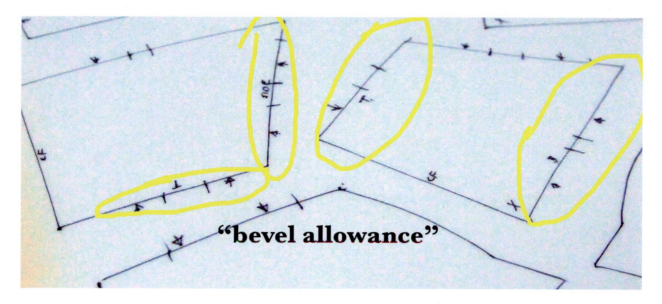

Figure 16-3: Adding a bevel allowance to foam pieces.

(Figure 16-4). If the precise size is not a concern, then there is no problem—leave the lines. When pattern pieces get numerous and complicated, the more lines and notes the better!

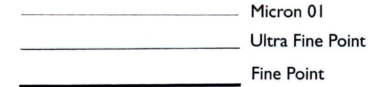

Micron 01

Ultra Fine Point

Fine Point

Figure 16-4: Width of marker lines.

To hold your patterns on the foam while tracing, use straight pins, T pins, pushpins, weights or whatever you find works best for you (Figure 16-5). The overall objective is that the pattern piece is stabilized while you carefully trace around the edges.

Figure 16-5: Patterns pinned to foam.

Transfer all notes and notches while tracing around each pattern (Figure 16-6). When the pattern has been traced, with all notations carefully transferred and printed on the foam, remove the paper piece.

Cutting Foam Pieces

Place the foam on a cutting surface. When cutting out foam pieces it may be easier to do a series of large cuts with scissors or a single-edged razor blade to free up the smaller pattern pieces before getting into detailed cuts. This will be easier with foam that is 1 inch or less.

Using a single-edged razor blade, cut along each side of the foam piece with a consistent, fluid movement. Try not to stop and start in the middle of a cut, this will result in a choppy edge. The goal is to get a clean, smooth edge so that the overall shape will not be distorted (Figure 16-6).

When cutting bevels hold the razor blade firmly at the proper angle. If you need two pieces of foam to form a 90-degree angle, both edges could be cut at 45 degrees, at 15 and 75 degrees, at 30 or 60 degrees, or any series of angles which will form the appropriate shape needed. Unless a matt cutter or a table saw can be modified to cut soft foam, the only way to custom bevel foam is by hand and with practice. As recommended previously cut out the large pieces first then cut the bevels as you begin to put the finished piece together. This way you can focus on the precise shape and figure out how the pieces need to be cut.

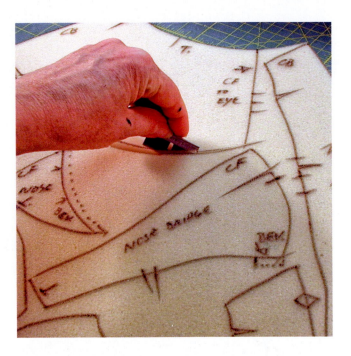

Figure 16-6: Cutting pattern pieces out with a razor blade.

Tip

When cutting out all the foam pieces, do the big cuts first, separating each piece before getting down to the details of beveling.

chapter seventeen

gluing and sewing

Before beginning to glue all the pieces together, lay out all the parts and mentally plan where the pieces go (Figure 17-1). Also have the paper patterns, the positive sculpture, and the foam mock-up close by to help if the pieces get a bit confusing.

While assembling the foam object, try cutting and gluing the beveled edges individually, a piece at time. For example, if working on a snout, I hold the pieces up in the general shape they will make together when assembled, and proceed to bevel each side. Then move on to the next connecting pieces. Remember an organic object could need many different bevels cut on one side alone so that it will contour and flow as the shape requires. Be patient, build a mock-up, and take your time when putting together the finished piece.

Gluing

Contact cement is commonly used (see *Chapter 1*) to stick foam pieces together. This adhesive is sturdy, dries fast (depending on the type), and lets the foam retain its flexibility.

Steps when using low VOC adhesives:

1. Apply a thin even coat to both surfaces. When applying use a scrap of foam. A thin even coat compared to a huge glob will help speed up the adhesion (Figure 17-2). I use a piece of scrap cardboard, dip my foam blotter into the adhesive, blot out the excess adhesive onto the cardboard, and then dab with a pecking motion, creating a thin, even film onto both surfaces (Figure 17-3).

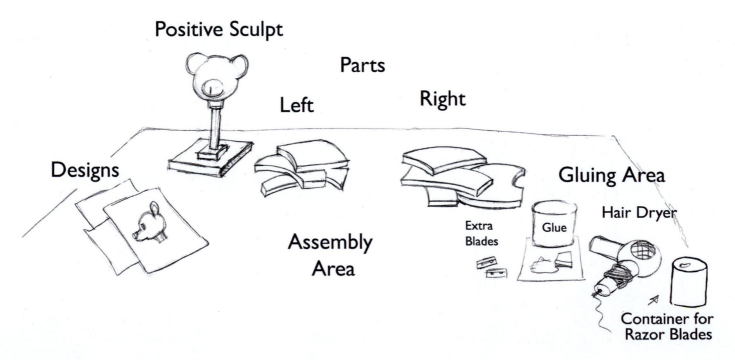

Figure 17-1: Assembly station set-up.

Figure 17-2: A thin coat of glue is best.

Figure 17-3: Gluing station set-up.

2. Use a hair dryer to speed up the drying time. Dry both surfaces until the adhesive becomes a translucent, cream color (the color will vary with adhesives) and is dry to the touch.
3. Press the foam together firmly and it should stick together. If it does not stick together give the area a few drying attempts with the hair dryer before applying more adhesive. An easy mistake to make is to assume the foam pieces are not sticking because there is not enough adhesive. Generally the real reason is that the adhesive is not dry and more adhesive will not help the situation. Students new to this adhesive will come to me saying, "It doesn't stick" or "It's not working". Their projects will often have many clotted layers of glue that have turned into a chunky mess. Again had they taken the time, the first layer would have probably worked.

The other side effect of too much adhesive (especially with the neoprene-based adhesives) is that the flexibility of the more porous foams can change, making them rigid. Less adhesive is more!

It is important to remember that different foams will require a slightly different amount of adhesive and drying time. Again there are foams with big pores and foams with no pores. The absorption and drying time will differ because of the variation of the surface.

Sewing

Some foams, such as polyester urethane reticulated foam (see Chapter 1), can be sewn and glued to create very attractive, sturdy pieces. You can sew darts, finish edges and sew features together by hand or on a machine using this foam (Figure 17-4). When sewing by hand a simple slip stitch in various widths can be used. To keep the knot from pulling through the porous foam, I will either use a small piece of fabric as a washer (to sew through) or I will knot the thread, pull it through the foam, and then draw the needle through the looped end thereby making a slip knot, which loops around the foam.

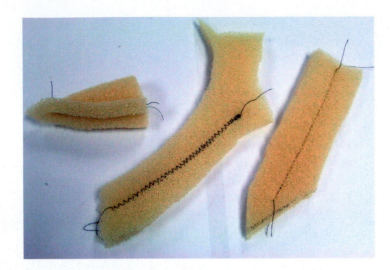

Figure 17-4: Sewn pieces reticulated foam. A sample of a machine-sewn dart, a zigzag, and a straight stitch.

SECTION VI

FINISHING THE DESIGN

chapter eighteen

fur and fabric coverings: selecting patterning, cutting, sculpting, and painting fun

A.

B.

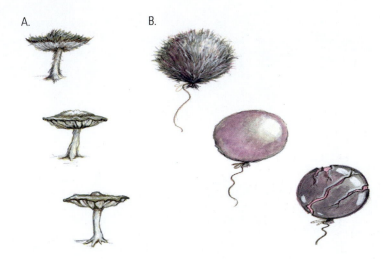

Figure 18-1: Three different textures.

A. Mushrooms.

B. Balloons.

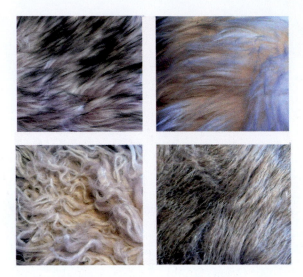

Figure 18-2: Different furs.

The choice of covering can be determined during or after the design process is complete. If a character design looks fuzzy, fluffy, bushy, and plush, then there is a good chance that it will be covered with fur. If a design seems soft, with a low, matt texture, then this could suggest a low-napped fur, antron fleece, or flocked fiber finish. If the design is shiny and hard looking yet needs to be flexible the option could be spandex, Lycra, or a rubber skin such as latex or neoprene (Figure 18-1).

Fur

When using fur as a covering there are many options to choose from. Not only are there a variety of lengths available but hundreds of textures and colors (Figure 18-2). For faux fur sources see *Appendices*).

Patterning Fur

When patterning a fabric covering such as fur, the first impulse might be to use the foam pattern used to make the foam object;

however the goal when using fur and any fabric covering is to keep seams to a minimum. When using a fabric with a nap such as fur a lot of seams can distort the direction of the fibers causing an otherwise sleek, plush finish to look nappy and rough (Figure 18-3).

Figure 18-3: Sewn fur covering.

To begin, think about how fur, hair, or facial hair grows, there is a definite direction and a natural flow. Observe fur/hair growth on animals.

Start with the design and pared-down shape to determine fur direction and placement.

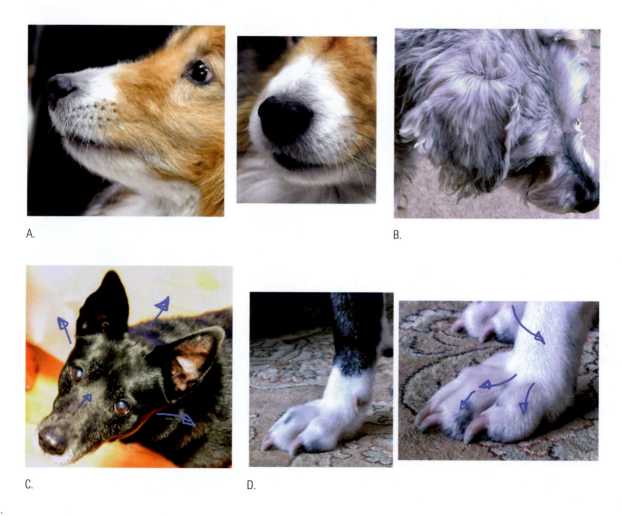

A.

B.

C.

D.

Figure 18-4:

A. Snout hair grows back and down towards the mouth and head.

B. Depending on the type of ear, outer ear hair grows up (or down) towards the tip of the ear.

C. Head hair grows back and down.

D. Paw hair grows down and back and runs down the leg towards the toes.

A.

B.

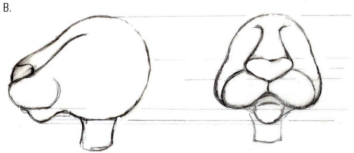

Figure 18-5: Tiger design.

A. Color rendering.

B. Pared-down, hairless foundation shape.

Start by draping the fabric on the front of the head or face, as this area needs to look the best because it is where attention will usually be focused (Figure 18-6).

If the foam object is symmetrical only one side needs to be draped. This will create a pattern that can be flipped or "cut on the fold". Determine the *center dividing line* and pin the fabric in place. As the fabric is smoothed over the object, excess folds can be pinched and pinned creating darts that help with contouring. Follow through with draping and pinning the entire half of the object. When all the darts have been pinned in place use a sharpie to mark where the pins connect—be certain to mark both sides of the fabric (Figure 18-7).

To indicate fur direction use arrows. This will help when the pattern is being laid out on the fur.

Patterning a "Break" or Color Change with Two or More Furs

If the design has two colors, then two different furs may need to be used (Figures 18-8 and 18-9). The "fur-color-break" can be indicated with drawn lines or by creating a deliberate draped "seam break".

To get the pattern needed to cut the appropriate shape, it is necessary to drape the foam object with a thin, sturdy fabric that is not thick like fur. Ordinary cotton muslin or something similar is commonly used.

Faux fur is a fibrous material available in various thicknesses that has a fabric foundation. The "draped muslin skin" represents the fabric foundation of the fur where the sewing will occur.

Before removing the draped fabric make certain all notes and notches have been put in place (Figure 18-10). It is possible to use the same notation system as used with the foam pieces, but label the fabric patterns specifically with terms such as "fur pattern" or "fabric skin" in case the foam and fabric patterns become mixed up.

Carefully remove the draped fabric pattern and lay out flat. Notice the marks where the darts were pinned (Figure 18-11).

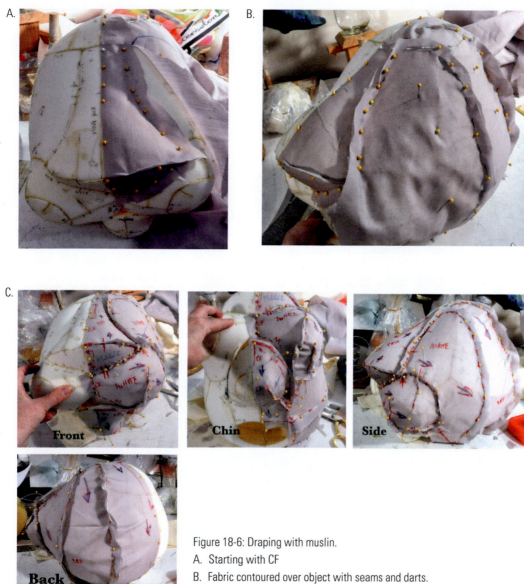

Figure 18-6: Draping with muslin.

A. Starting with CF

B. Fabric contoured over object with seams and darts.

C. Muslin skin trimmed and finished with notes.

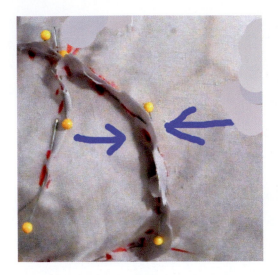

Figure 18-7: Marking both sides of the pinned seams and darts to indicate where the pins join.

Figure 18-8: Patterning a color break. Yellow indicates where the white fur will be.

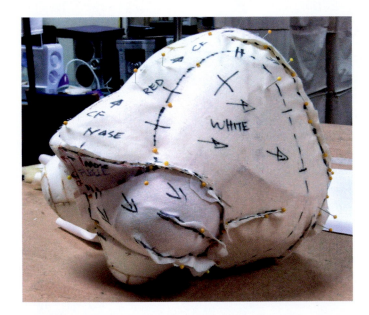

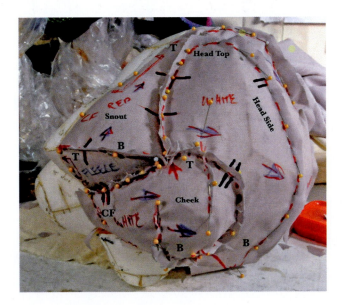

Figure 18-9: Another example of a different muslin draped on the same head. Notice that the dart placement is slightly different.

Figure 18-10: Final note and notch layout on muslin.

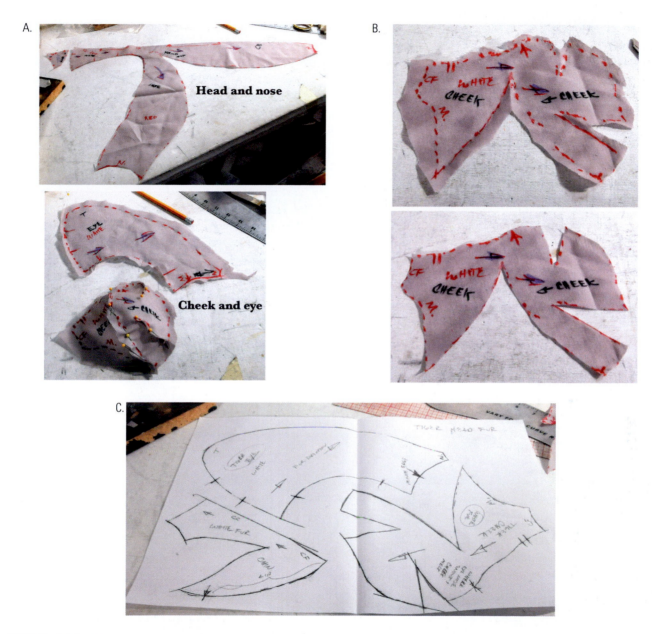

Figure 18-11: The fabric pattern.

A. Parts of the fabric pattern spread flat.

B. Cutting out darts and cleaning up edges.

C. Transfer fabric pattern to paper and clean up edges with a ruler.

Use a ruler and pencil to clean up the lines on the fabric. Following the pencil lines, trim off seam allowances and the excess fabric left in the darts. The remaining shape is the pattern for the fur. Transfer the fabric pattern to paper, then "true-up" the pieces with a ruler and pencil. See *Chapter 11*.

Laying Out Pattern on Fur

To determine the fur direction or "nap" of the fur, hold the fur up in the air and shake slightly in different directions. This will help settle the fibers in the direction they need to lie. The *selvage edge* or the factory edges running down the long sides of the fur can also help when determining fur direction, e.g. the fur nap can be parallel to the selvage edge, but this is not always the case. Some fur can lie on the *bias* or diagonal of the fabric. It can also lay *cross-grain* or perpendicular to the selvage edge (Figure 18-12). Because the direction of the fur can get a little confusing when it is upside down lying on a table, it is

sometimes helpful to draw an arrow on the wrong side of the fabric to help indicate the direction. This is especially true with fur over 1 inch in length.

Lay out the pattern pieces on the wrong side of the fabric, keeping in mind the fur direction. Pin the pieces in place and using a marker, carefully trace around the shapes (Figure 18-13).

> ## Tip
> Just like regular fabric, some faux fur fabric can have the nap of the fur laying "cross grain" or be woven on the bias. This will make a difference when it comes to how the fur fabric will stretch and hug the shape of whatever the object will be. Fur fabric on the bias will stretch the most.

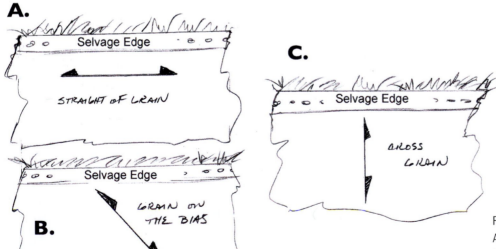

Figure 18-12: Faux fur fabric weave.
A. With the grain or parallel to the selvage edge.
B. On the bias or diagonal to the selvage edge.
C. Cross-grain or perpendicular to the selvage edge.

A.

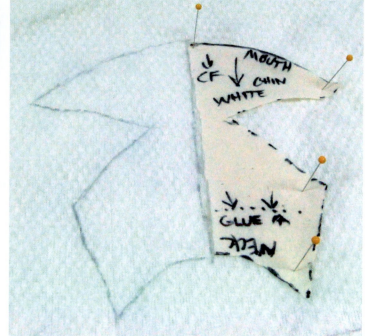

C.

B.

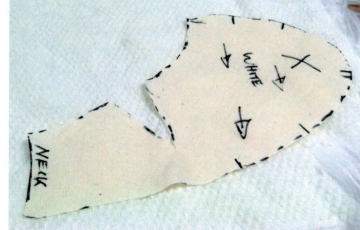

D.

Figure 18-13:

A. Muslin draped parts removed.

B. Parts trimmed.

C. Pattern lying out on fur. Notice that it has been flipped.

D. Note the fur direction when laying out the patterns.

With the exception of the areas where major seam allowances are necessary to wrap around an edge such as necks and mouths, the seam allowances on these pieces should be 1/4 inch or less. Seam allowances can cause bulk and the more bulk underneath the skin the less well it will hug the foam contours. I have a tendency to err on the side of caution and leave 1/2-inch seam allowances but these always get cut away. *Note*: remember to flip the pattern pieces while maintaining the direction of the fur and repeat the tracing process for the opposite side.

Cutting Fur

One of the advantages of using a material like fur and antron fleece is that the seams can be hidden. Care should be taken to not cut the loose fur fibers. If the fur fibers are left undamaged along the edges of seams, then after the pieces are sewn together, the fibers can be gently teased out (Figure 18-14).

Tip

I rarely if ever use scissors to cut fur. Scissors are faster but can create a blunt, "factory edge" which can completely deaden the natural look of fur and inhibit the ability of the fur fibers to hide seams.

Make an incision in the back of the fur fabric with a razor blade or an x-acto knife, then hold up the fabric and slice only the woven fabric foundation. After the pieces have been cut out, brush the fur away from the edges and pin each together. The pieces can be sewn by hand, or on a sewing machine using a straight or zigzag stitch. A serged edge may also work but make certain the fur fibers are out of the way of the serger blade or you will have lost the ability to hide the seam.

Rough Fit

After the majority of the pieces have been sewn together, do a "rough fit" on the foam piece. Some seam areas may need to be released to get the fur skin on the object, then hand-stitched in place. This is also a good time to tell if excess seam allowances should be removed (Figure 18-14).

Now replace the fur skin, and stitch closed. *Note*: if deciding to use glue on the fur be very sparing because you may need to stitch through it later. Some dried adhesives are difficult to stitch through.

Using a comb or a pin, lightly but vigorously tease the matted fur out of the stitched seams. If the fur was left uncut then the seams will disappear beautifully!

Tip

If the fur seams look irregular or a bit "off grain", it is possible to comb, style, and *fix* the fur with a little hairspray to make it look more fluid and natural. A light steaming with a clothing steamer may help direct the fibers as well.

Sculpting and Trimming Fur

When I used fur for the first time as a covering, I was horrified because all of the careful contouring I built into the foam piece was completely concealed by the great mass of fluff. It was a shaggy shrub of fibers! But as I soon learned, one of the wonderful benefits of using fur is that it can be combed and styled, and contoured over shapes by trimming. Fur can also be enhanced with longer tufts of feathers, fake hair, and longer fur to add additional depth.

Trimming and sculpting can be done with small scissors or very carefully with shears to reveal details of the face and enhance contours of the body (Figure 18-17). Make sure to experiment with fur samples before jumping into the actual

Figure 18-14: Cutting and sewing fur.

A. Cutting with a razor blade.

B. Brush fur away from the seam edges and pin together.

C. Sample sewn on a machine with a zigzag stitch and a straight stitch, and also on a serger. Fur can also be sewn by hand.

D. Teasing out fur fibers.

E. Pattern transferred to fur.

F. Fur shape cut out.

G. Fur serged together to form a hood.

Figure 18-15:
A. Rough fit of hood.
B. Attaching the entire head covering then handsewing up the back.

A.

B.

Figure 18-16:
A. Before adding fur.
B. After fur is added.

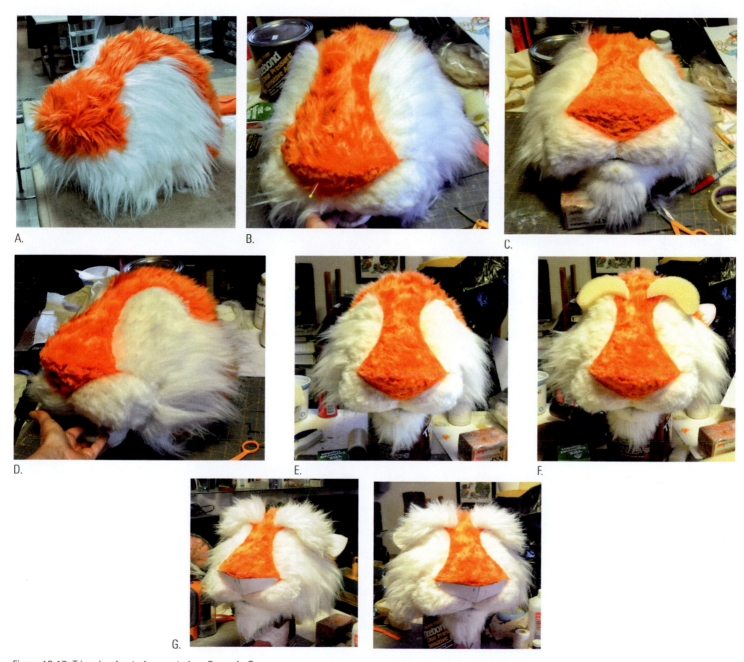

Figure 18-17: Trimming fur; before and after. Steps A–G.

A.

B.

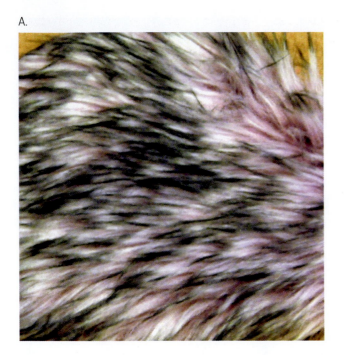

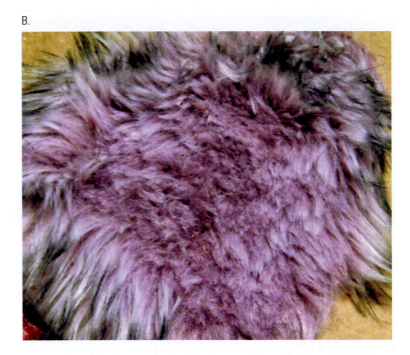

Figures 18-18A and B: Sample of fur before and after trimming showing two-toned fibers.

piece. Some fur is tipped or two-toned, meaning the fur ends can be a different color than the base and if cut away it could look dramatically different (Figure 18-18).

Dying Fur

Fake fur is made of plastic fibers and as far as changing the color is concerned, it is much better to buy it pre-dyed. In the past it was only possible to dye fur using acetate/nylon or polyester dye, steaming water, a respirator, goggles, gloves, and patience and if the foundation color of the fur was white, brilliant custom colors could be achieved. However, recently manufacturers have begun to produce different types of fur with fiber content that can take *some* color with acid or Rit Dyes. This type of fur is sold as 100 percent polyester but either the poly fibers are a type that absorbs dye or there must be

Figure 18-19: Fur that has been tinted with dye.

some nylon fibers present (Figure 18-19). Again it is important to always do a test to make certain that the fiber content is what it claims to be.

Tests should be made to see how the fur reacts with the dye and if the texture of the fur changes at very high temperatures. Some fluffy, soft fur can turn into matted, frizzy, singed chunks if the heat is too high. So care should be taken before leaping in to this stage of the process.

Antron Fleece

Antron fleece (not to be confused with *polar fleece*) is a great fabric covering for foam. It is best known for its use on puppets.

The finished look is a rich, matt, soft surface that absorbs light really well. Fleece stretches, dyes well with union (Rit brand) and acid dyes, but its best-known quality is that when sewn properly, the seams will disappear. It is similar to fur in that the fibers of antron fleece can be teased out to cover the trough created by seams and stitches (Figure 18-20).

Fleece fabric can be brushed out and shaved down to remove some of the fuzzy thickness that can turn into small, nappy balls with friction and wear. The result of shaving fleece is a creamy finish that is lovely. However, if the fleece is trimmed too short, it limits the fabric's ability to hide seams as effectively.

Figure 18-20: Antron fleece.
A. Hand stitching on fleece.
B. Machine stitching.
C. A picked or teased seam.
D. A comparison of unshaved fleece and shaved fleece.

Tip

When using stretch fabrics such as antron fleece, spandex, stretch pleather, Lycra, and velour, it is recommended that a stretch fabric be used to drape the mock-up pattern. However, this is the only variation on the draping process; the same steps as mentioned when draping fur apply to the rest of the draping process. See the section on "Patterning fur".

Figure 18-21: Spandex ghoul lips.

Additional Fabric Coverings

Foam can be covered with any fabric provided it retains the quality needed for the desired movement. Slick and velvety fabrics such spandex, Lycra, velour, and stretch pleather are all options though the seams can be distracting if not strategically placed or hidden with trim (Figure 18-21).

Other coverings such as latex and tissue, latex and pantyhose, or cheesecloth and flex glue are all great ways to add a covering to foam surfaces (Figure 18-22)

A.

B.

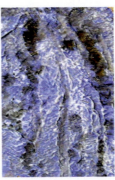

C.

Figure 18-22:
A. Cheesecloth and flex glue.

B. Latex and tissue.
C. Polyether foam painted with latex and airbrushed.

chapter nineteen

uncovered foam: how to finish

Uncovered foam as a finished texture can also be a successful option depending on the design. If looking for a matte, soft, porous finish, then open-celled urethane foam (reticulated or upholstery) is the way to go. If the finished surface is smooth or highly detailed with carvings, then closed-cell foam is the best bet.

Open-cell reticulated foam can be dyed or painted, and is tough enough to go without a fabric covering (Figure 19-2). The finish is porous and can add an intriguingly spongy texture to finished pieces. Though not as durable, open-celled upholstery foam can also be dyed.

Figure 19-1

Figure 19-2: The finished look of porous foam.

Dying Foam

Using dye as a means of coloring foam is much better than paint. Paint only sits on the surface layer, whereas dye goes all the way through the foam and becomes intrinsic to the piece. Paint can also make foam stiff when too thick. Dye, on the other hand, since it is a stain, will maintain the flexibility of the foam.

Both of these urethane foams dye well with acid dyes. Reticulated foam can be pot dyed or dyed in a washing machine. If using upholstery foam, stick with pot dying as the agitator in the washing machine could tear the foam.

How to Dye Open-Celled Urethane, Reticulated Foam

The washing machine is not recommended for dying upholstery foam. *Note:* wear the appropriate safety gear with this process. This includes goggles, long gloves, an apron, and a respirator.

1. Fill a washing machine with hot water or heat a large pot. The water does not need to be steaming hot.

Tip

It is possible to make a watered down "paint tea" and stain foam. Use the same method as that used for dying thick pieces of foam. The paint water should be squeezed though the foam. When dry this process could still stiffen the foam slightly.

2. After testing for the appropriate color, add desired amount of dye to water and mix thoroughly. If using a washing machine, let it mix for approximately 1 minute. If using a large pot, mix with a long stick or dye spoon, until all the particles are dissolved.

Tip

Around a yard of 1-inch foam, at 60 inches wide, is the maximum size for a full washing machine. If using 1/4-inch to 5/8-inch foam, more can be dyed. Remember: dye formulas are usually calculated by the amount of dye per pound of fabric, but foam weighs next to nothing, therefore err on the side of less dye because foam absorbs dye/color very well. Smaller amounts of dye added in stages to achieve the correct color is the way to go.

Tip

No matter what kind of foam is being used, if too much foam is crammed into the washer, the agitator could score it. Less is better.

3. If dying thick pieces of reticulated foam (over 1 inch), use a dye pot. While wearing a pair of gloves, squish and squeeze the foam to work the dye through the thickness of the foam. Work fast because the dye will absorb into the first thing it touches, which is the surface. Reticulated foam is designed to be used for filtration so get the water moving into and through it fast!
4. Thoroughly rinse out any dye not absorbed, then squeeze or spin out any excess water in the machine.

5. It is best to lay the foam flat or hang it to dry. Putting sheets in a hot or warm dryer could add permanent creases.

Tip

Try dying pre-cut pattern pieces instead of whole sheets.

Painting Foam

Closed-Cell Foam

While not good for dying because it is waterproof, closed-cell foam is smooth and non-porous and is excellent for painting with acrylic, latex, or "pax" paint, using an airbrush or a paintbrush. It can be sealed with translucent or clear sealers such as *Flex Glue*, *Sculpt or Coat*, or *Modpodge* to give a shiny or matte finish. Latex, neoprene, and any number of other options can be used to add various finishes to this foam as well.

Figure 19-3: Heat curled 1/4-inch L 200 on cold foam mask, used for hair.

If glued seam edges are a little uneven, *Extra Fast Setting Drywall Spackle* can be used to patch and smooth them over. Then a sealer such as *Sculpt or Coat* can be sponged or painted on. The finish painting done with acrylic paint can produce objects that are lightweight and professional looking.

Tip

Remember that one of the great characteristics of *closed-cell foam* is that it can be manipulated with heat. Heat manipulation is not technically a "finish", yet some interesting effects can be achieved nonetheless (Figure 19-3). Remember to use safe practices when heating foam (see *Chapter 2*).

Painting

Painting with an Airbrush and Preval Sprayers

Figure 19-4: Double action airbrush.

The airbrush is a handy tool. It can be used for adding shear, translucent layers of paint like a dustcoat, or it can be used to apply opaque layers of color. If painting open–celled urethane foam or closed–cell foam, airbrushing is one really good way to apply color. It is possible to maintain some of the flexibility of foam if the layers of paint stay very thin. Use a hair dryer to speed up the drying process. However, the best use of the airbrush is as a finish tool for adding subtle color to creases and folds. See *Chapter 20*.

A Preval sprayer is canned air with a small glass jar attached to pick up liquid and spray it. Unlike the airbrush, which needs an air compressor and the airbrush itself needs to be cleaned thoroughly while using to keep it working properly, this type of sprayer is more mobile and therefore handier to use in the field. The canned air is CFC free and recyclable as well. It can be used to spray paint and dye.

Though not advised, dye can also be used with an airbrush to add contours and subtle colors. Remember when putting paint or dye through an airbrush you are turning it into an airborne particulate so be sure to use the appropriate safety equipment. See *Chapter 2*.

Hand Painting

Hand painting using brushes and sponges is a good way to apply color to foam. Closed-cell foam or L 200 is the best foam for hand painting though color can be rubbed on and into open-celled urethane foam as well.

A.

B.

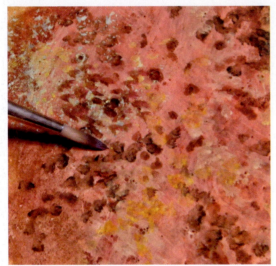

C.

Figure 19-5: Painting techniques on foam.

A. **Dry brushing**. Laying on a foundation color, letting it dry, then lightly dragging another color (tint or shade) over the top to hit any details. When adding a lighter tone on top of the foundation color this is called a *highlight*. The highlight adds lighter tones to areas to raise them visually. A highlighted area will draw attention to itself. It can be used to great effect on wrinkles and other protuberant areas. The "dry brush technique" is a great technique for this effect. The term *lowlight* is the opposite of highlight in that a painted shadow is added at the base of protuberant areas.

B. **Wet blending.** Painting with a variety of colors while still wet to give a blended, mottled look.

C. **Stippling**. Using a pointed brush with a round metal ferrule (called a "round"), to dab individual colors in small dots or swipes. Stippling can be a great effect if using a variety of colors. See paintings of Georges Seurat.

The ultimate wet blend

chapter twenty

detailing and bringing to life

Figure 20-1: "Arnie the Twisk" design.

The final finishing steps are often the most critical when bringing a character, an object, or anything that is custom made to life. Unfortunately this step is often rushed or skipped because either time has not been allotted or because the item is "good enough, box it, and get it out of here!" The *detailing* is the twinkle in the eye, the icing on the cake, the crud painted on the teeth, the shading airbrushed around the eyes, the sprigs of hair added to a mole, or any of a dozen other final cosmetic particulars that can individualize the finished object.

Hair

Ways to Attach Hair and Apply Hair and Fur

Long wisps and tufts of fur, plastic, fabric, or feathers are all great materials to help add depth when finalizing. Along with the lush look of the additional textures, the object's *movement* can also be enhanced subtly. Sometimes magic can happen when the puppet or prop is motionless, yet air currents still move the fringe or feathers decorating it like sea fronds.

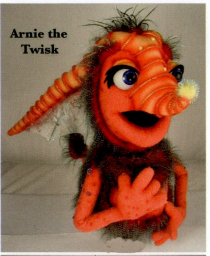

Figure 20-2: Adding longer pieces of fur, fake and real hair, and feathers can enhance features and contours.

There are various ways to add wisps (feathers, long fur tufts, hair, etc.) into fur foundations.

1. **Glue.** One good way is by gluing individual hairs or prepared clumps. Decide and prepare the area where the hair or feathers will be added by separating the fibers on the fur till the foundation fabric is visible (Figure 20-3). Then gather a small clump of hair or feathers to be added. Trim the ends evenly,

A.

B.

C.

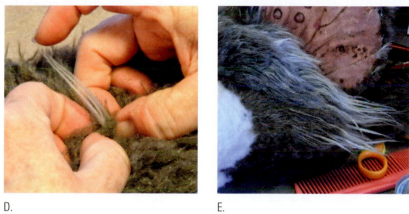

D.

E.

Figure 20-3:

A. Foundation fur before adding.

B. Trimming hair to be glued.

C. Adding adhesive to fur ends—in this case hot glue.

D. Adding hair and teasing fibers together with fingers.

E. Final look after combing and styling.

A.

B.

Figure 20-4: Hand tie directly into fur.
A. Prepping hole with ventilating needle and pulling fiber through.
B. Finished with added fiber.

and touch or rub a small amount of hot glue (do not squeeze a big glob of glue onto the fur foundation or onto the gathered feathers) or other quick setting adhesive onto the tips. Place the glued tips against the fabric base of the separated fibers in the direction or angle at which you want the hair to seem to grow. Then, before the glue cools or sets, tease the base fur into the adhesive and hair just added. Do not press the fur down into the glue, but encourage it with fingertips or pins to integrate and stand up straight. Repeating this process can make an area look full and fluffy. A great effect!

2. **Hand tying.** An equally good way to add hair is by tying the hair into the foundation material. The terms *latch-hook, hand tie*, or *ventilate* all basically mean to insert and knot hair or fibers directly into the fur, fabric, or netting foundation (Figure 20-4).

3. **Punching hair.** The term *punching hair* means to force a fiber or hair into the foundation of the object. When done correctly it can look as if it is literally growing out of the surface. The hair or fiber is caught in the cleft of a small tool such as the eye of a needle that's been clipped open, and then inserted or poked into the surface material. When the tool is removed the hair stays in place because the force of the foundation material traps it. *Note*: this technique works more successfully when punching into foundations such as silicone, latex, and backed closed-cell foam. The gooey or clinging quality of these materials helps to hold the fibers in place.

The technique of hand tying fibers into fabric net is used for making latch-hook rugs and ventilated (hand-tied) wigs. With the exception of the scale and the kinds of materials used, both techniques are basically the same. The technique uses a tiny slip knot tied through the foundation fabric.

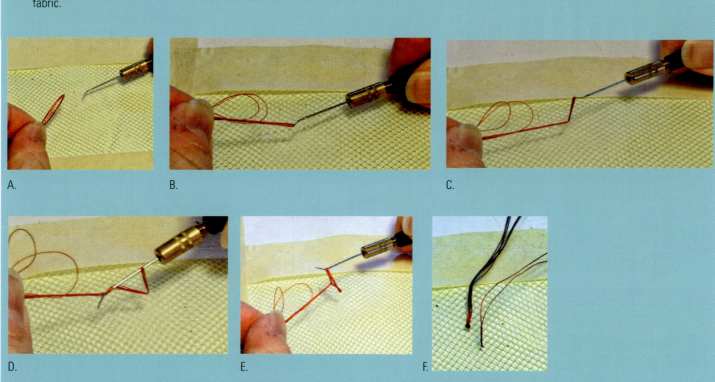

A.   B.   C.

D.   E.   F.

Figure 20-5: Hand tying fibers. How to hand tie fibers. The example uses sewing thread.

A. Make a loop with fibers.

B. Hook a few fibers as needed with tool.

C. Pull through netting.

D. Grab fibers again.

E. Pull through loop.

F. Finished, cinched-in fiber. The fewer fibers/hairs that are hooked the smaller the knot.

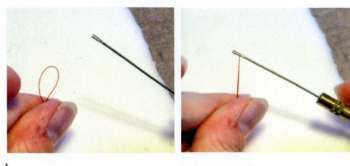

A.

B.

C.

D.

Painting Hair and Fur

Adding painted details is a very good way of enhancing color and depth on a newly built object. Airbrushing and hand painting with brushes are good ways of tinting and shading.

Fur can be tinted by airbrushing, by using a mist of spray hair color, or with spray paints like those produced by the Design Master company which are designed to dust-coat faux silk foliage. One of the great qualities of fur is that the longer varieties, just like feathers, will move with air currents. If too much paint is added that quality can easily be lost because the paint will weigh down the fibers. This is not necessarily bad for every situation when using fur. Sometimes a heavily styled fur, wherein the fur is posed with fixative to keep its shape, lends itself to being painted.

Figure 20-6: Punching hair.

A. Modify a sewing needle with a large eye by clipping it open. Then make a loop with the fiber and slip it into the open eye.

B. Press loaded tool into prepped area and remove tool pulling straight up.

C. Several threads punched into foam. Can secure on the backside by adding adhesive.

D. Sample of punched horsehair.

Figure 20-7: Different products that can be used for tinting synthetic and organic fibers: design master spray paints, liquid chalk hair color, leather dye or fabric dyes for feathers, colored mousse and spray hair color, paint-on hair color applied with brush, acrylic or latex paint, chalk pastels.

Much of the fluffiness of fur can still be preserved by laying on very light layers of paint and then blow-drying and brushing between each layer. The fibers will want to mat together so the emphasis here is placed on *multiple, very light layers* of paint.

Paint and also temporary hair colors can be brushed into fur using stiff bristled paintbrushes, toothbrushes, and even bristled mascara wands. Make sure to experiment on sample pieces of fur before jumping in. However, the possibilities are really endless.

Other fabrics such as antron fleece, spandex, and raw foam can be contour painted and detailed by using an airbrush or floral spray. Chalk pastels can also be used to lightly tint areas on fleece and raw urethane foam with a make-up applicator.

Adding Sparkle

Glitter has a dicey reputation, often being associated with cheap crafts or cheesy production values. But glitter and paint with glitter suspended in it, if used properly, can make an object look sparkly, shiny, sweaty, or greasy. Glitter comes in basically three sizes: large flakes, common, medium-sized flakes, and micro-sized flakes. Depending on the venue any of these can work but of the three varieties I prefer the micro-sized or ultra-fine glitter (Figure 20-8). I use it as an addition in eyes, on fur,

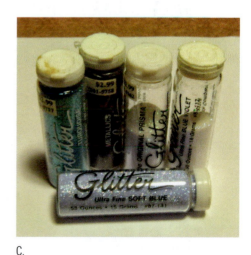

A.

B.

C.

Figure 20-8: Glitter.

A. Sample skin from a distance. The greasy quality is from micro glitter.

B. Puff paint.

C. Micro glitter.

skin, and any place where there needs to be added depth or twinkle to a mere glossy surface.

Adding Other Details

Additional details that can be added are: teeth, horns, fingernails, warts, pustules, freckles, dots, irises, pupils, and nostril hair . . . the list goes on and on. These can either be two-dimensionally painted or three-dimensional embellishments (which I prefer) made with L 200, polyethylene plastic, friendly plastic, fingernail polish, found objects (such as plastic grapes or random plastic shapes) . . . and this list too goes on and on.

Finishing Touches

SECTION VII

THIS SECTION GOES THROUGH THE FULL PROCESS FOR SIX PROJECTS

chapter twenty-one

free-form foam construction

Open-cell foam (reticulated) was used for this project; however closed-cell foam (L 200) could also be used.

Figure 21-1: Begin with a rectangle roughly 18 inches by 10 inches.

Figure 21-2: Make a tube by gluing the two short sides together.

Figure 21-3: Divide the top of the cylinder into four sections by adding marks. Between the marks at the top of the cylinder, measure down 4–5 inches and make another mark. Make four cuts from the top down to those marks. The rough shape shown here was drawn in before cutting.

Figure 21-4: Connect the top set of dots down to the lower set by sketching slightly curved lines and cuts, this will create darts.

Figure 21-5: Glue the sides of each dart and the end will round off.

Figure 21-7: Glue all the darts except the bottom two. This allows for a mouth.

A.

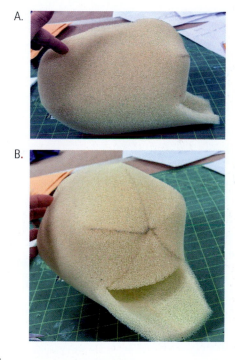

B.

Figure 21-6: At the opposite end add only three darts. These will be shallower darts and do not go all the way around this end of the cylinder. See Figures 21-8A and B.

Figure 21-8:
A. Notice the slightly rounded end when the shallower dart is used.
B. Fill in opening with two triangular pieces. The lower edge is left uncut until the shape is decided.

Figure 21-9: To make the mouth bigger, extend the incisions at the sides 1 or 2 inches further back. A deeper mouth can add ease of movement when manipulating.

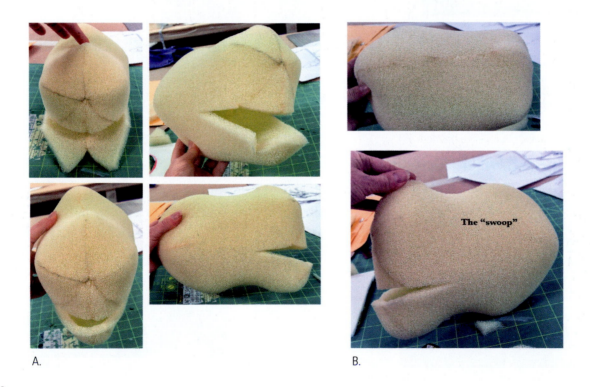

The "swoop"

A.   B.

Figure 21-10:
A. Cut a smaller dart at center to create a slightly different contour in the lower jaw.
B. Add a slight swoop on the bridge of the nose by cutting out an oval and gluing it closed again. See *Figure 9-12*.

Figure 21-11: Pattern and make a mouth plate out of leather, felt, or foam and glue in place.

Figure 21-12:
A. Add glue to the edges of the shapes and glue the edges down to round them out.
B. Glue rough c shapes for the nostrils, then carve with scissors.
C. Make paper patterns for the ears to get a sense of size.

Figure 21-13: Cut out two foam ears using a pattern. Make a small incision in the back of the head and glue the ears in place.

Figure 21-14: Line mouth with felt and glue with contact cement. Airbrush a light blue color over the entire head. Let dry, then add shading to any protuberant features and inside the mouth.

Figure 21-15: Eyes are made of thin disks of yellow 1/8-inch thick fun foam
(L 200) mounted with black buttons painted with black gloss spray paint.

Figure 21-17: Finished blue rhino.

Figure 21-16: The reticulated foam horn was exchanged for a patterned L 200
then contour painted.

chapter twenty-two

making two different shapes from the same foam pattern

Open-cell foam (reticulated) was used for this project; however closed-cell foam could also be used.

A.

B.

Figure 22-1: Start with the design.

A. Mouse.

B. Mongoose with profile sketch.

Figure 22-2: Create a positive sculpt.

ear mock-up

Figure 22-3: Create a preliminary paper mock-up for mouse's ear.

Figure 22-4: Add four coats of latex to positive sculpt.

Figure 22-5: Dividing up the shape with lines to determine the pattern pieces.

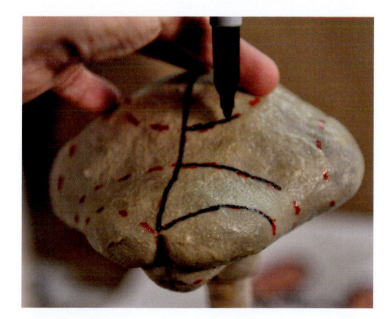

Figure 22-6: Confirming choices with a black sharpie.

Figure 22-7: Adding notations and notches.

Figure 22-8: Cutting off half the skin.

Figure 22-9: Dusting latex with baby powder and removing half of the skin.

Figure 22-10: Cutting apart the shapes.

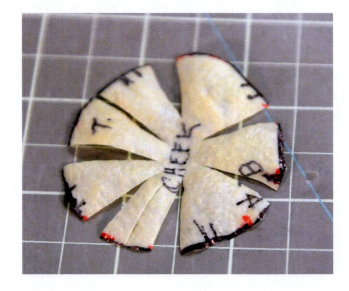

Figure 22-11: Discovering darts with the slash and spread method.

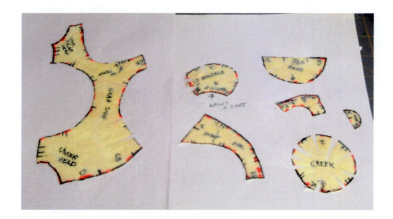

Figure 22-12: Taping pieces to paper.

Figure 22-14: Copying and enlarging pieces 154 percent.

Figure 22-13: Scaling pieces to desired size by measuring the sculpt width and height.

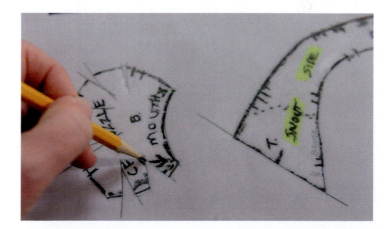

Figure 22-15: Cleaning up darts with ruler and pencil.

Figure 22-16: Cutting out the pieces and laying them out on foam. Don't forget to flip them!

Figure 22-17: All pieces cut out.

Figure 22-18: Gluing all the darts together on each piece before assembling the entire shape.

Figure 22-19: Assembling big pieces.

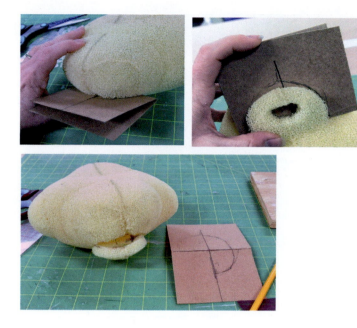

Figure 22-20: Patterning a mouth plate.

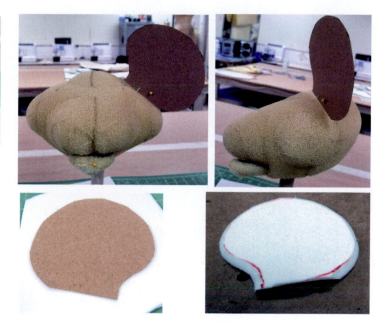

Figure 22-22: Looking again at ear pattern and cutting it out of L 200.

Figure 22-21: Small added piece to chin that will be carved with scissors.

Figure 22-23: Mouse and mongoose side by side. Mouse head shape slightly different because of cut angle. Mongoose has a wider mouth and is still without mouth plate.

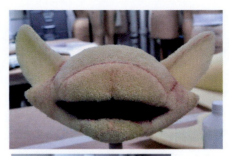

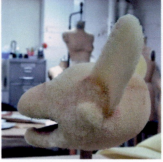

Figure 22-24: Added foam to mongoose forehead and cheeks.

Figure 22-26: Added carved mongoose ears.

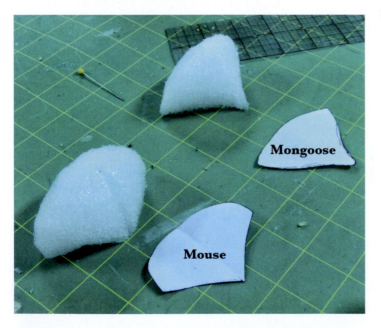

Figure 22-25: Two different shaped noses: mouse and mongoose.

Figure 22-27: First layer of yellow paint, also tinting of mouth felt liner.

Figure 22-28: Adding darker yellow and brown contour colors and additional accent painting.

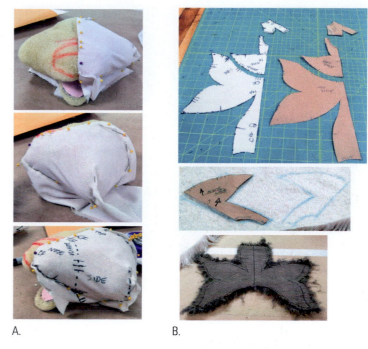

A.

B.

Figure 22-30:
A. Draping fur pattern on mouse.
B. Creating pattern, laying out, and cutting fur.

Figure 22-29: Attaching mongoose nose, brows, and eyes.

Figure 22-31: Sewing and putting on mouse head.

Figure 22-32: Combing and trimming fur.

Figure 22-33: Attaching ears and brows.

Figure 22-34: Styling and detailing with fur tufts and ears.

Figure 21-35: Painting and attaching mouse nose.

Figure 22-36: Adding teeth, painting, and any final details.

Figure 22-37: Finished mouse.

Figure 22-38: Finished mongoose.

chapter twenty-three

patterned foam mask

Closed-cell foam (L 200) was used for this project; however open-celled foam could also be used.

Figure 23-1: Start with design.

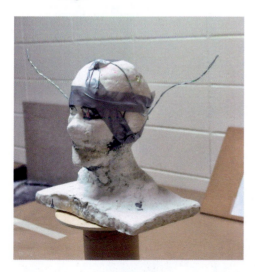

Figure 23-2: Sculpt the positive on a plaster head form to get the exact scale. Add wire to head form to support the clay.

Figure 23-3: Roughing in clay form and constantly looking at the sculpt from all angles.

Figure 23-4: Finished sculpt profile and front view.

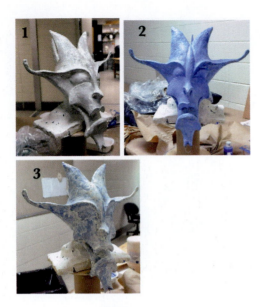

Figure 23-5: Coating with layers of slip casting latex.

1. First layer is plain latex sponged on.
2. Second layer is tinted with latex paint.
3. Third layer is plain latex again.

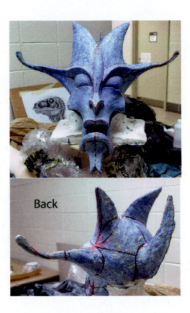

Figure 23-7: Sketching in patterns lines and transferring lines around entire head.

Figure 23-6: Adding center dividing line with red sharpie.

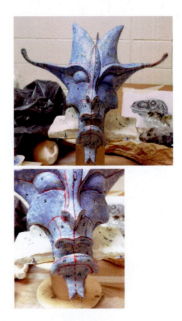

Figure 23-8: Numbering pattern pieces.

A.

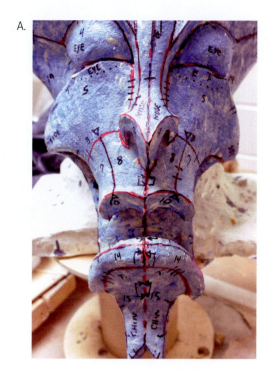

B.

Figure 23-10: Cutting off skin in pieces. *Note*: only removing half of the skin from sculpt.

Figure 23-9A and B: Confirming line choices with a black sharpie and adding notches to indicate specific connection and placement. *Note*: both sides get symmetrical notation.

Figure 23-11: Pieces separated, darted, then taped to sheets. *Note*: each sheet contains specific areas, e.g. ears, lower jaw, etc.

Figure 23-13: All paper pattern pieces transferred to foam. Each piece has been flipped to allow for both sides of the object. *Note*: the "bevel allowances" accommodated for during pattern layout for future beveling.

Figure 23-12: Sheets copied for truing up with pencil and ruler. *Note*: since piece was sculpted at life size no scaling was necessary.

Figure 23-14: All parts cut out and divided into piles: lower front, upper front, and back.

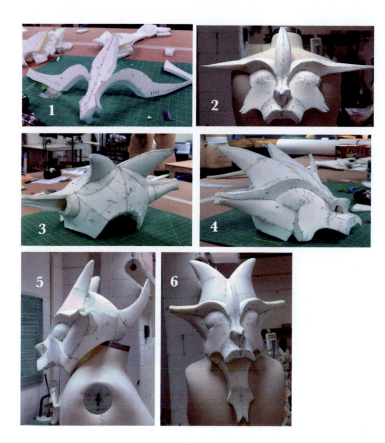

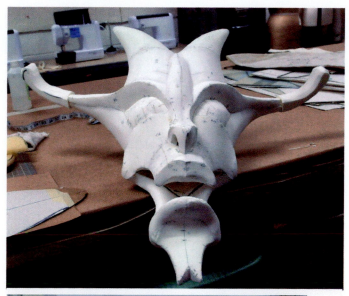

Figure 23-15: Assembling parts.

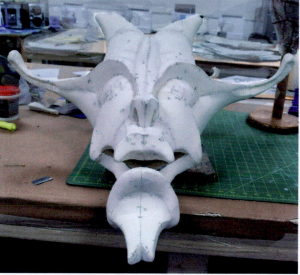

Figure 23-16: Ear tips were carved and sanded pieces of mini-cell foam mounted on rods and added separately.

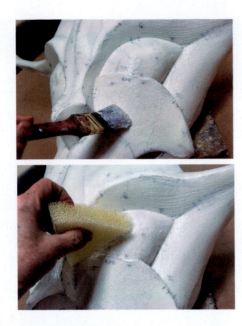

Figure 23-17: After spackling any irregularities with *Extra Fast Setting Drywall Spackle* and lightly sanding, brush on a thick layer of *sculpt* or *coat*. Using a reticulated foam scrap, stipple over wet medium to eliminate brush strokes. Repeated three times.

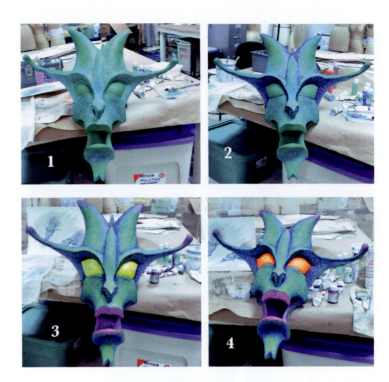

Figure 23-18: Painting layers.

Figure 23-19: Black shank button pupils added.

Figure 23-20: Finished mask with wig attached.

chapter twenty-four

patterned foam armor

Closed-cell foam (L 200) was used for this project.

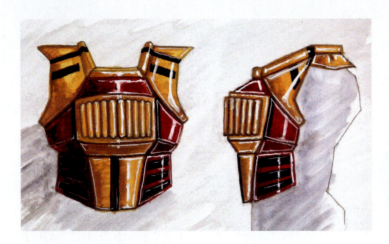

Figure 24-1: Start with a design.

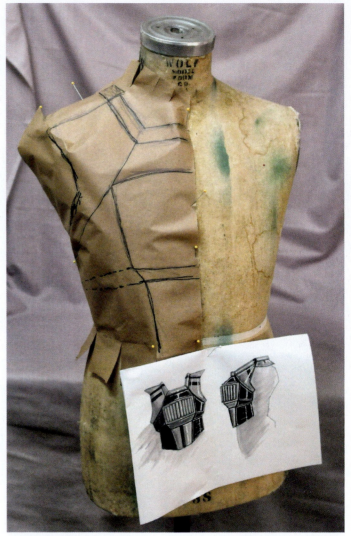

Figure 24-2: Create the pattern of the armor directly on a dress form or scale using steps in Chapters 12–14.

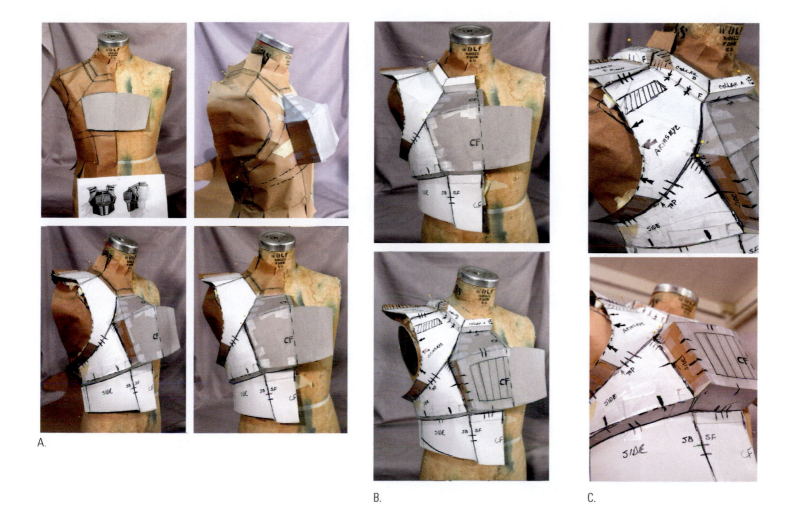

Figure 24-3: Cardboard armor mock-up built on a paper foundation. This will help to determine rough shapes.

A. Roughing in shapes.

B. Finishing collar and adding notes.

C. Adding final notches and labels.

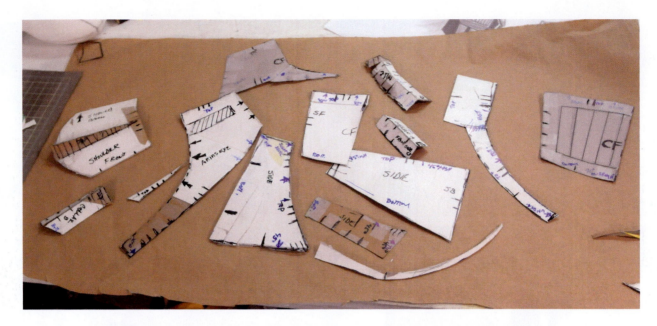

Figure 24-4: All parts removed and laid out flat.

Figure 24-5: All pieces transferred to paper and trued-up. Sides needing beveling indicated with pink highlighter.

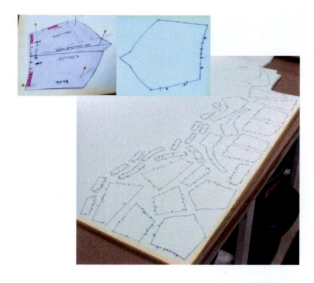

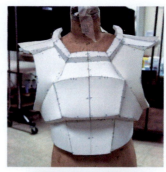

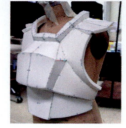

Figure 24-6: Laying paper patterns on L 200 foam and transferring lines. *Note*: remember to flip patterns.

B.

C.

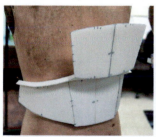

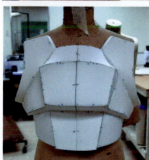

A.

Figure 24-7: Assembling parts from bottom up because the top is more complex.

A. Bottom and sides.

B. Collar and epaulets.

C. Detail on center plate with ethyfoam rod.

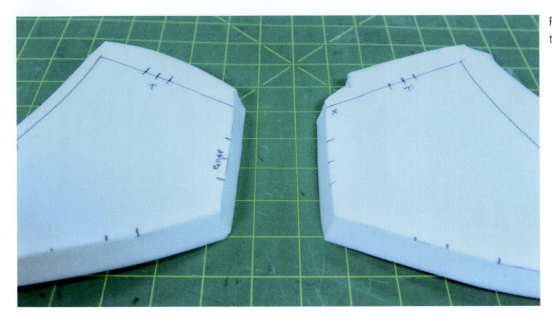

Figure 24-8: Sample of beveled cuts. Cut the bevel for each joint as it is assembled.

Figure 24-9: Three layers of *Plasti Dip* as a primer coat which also fortifies the foam. Each layer is allowed to dry between every brushed-on application. The brush strokes will be visible using this primer. It is, however, possible to hand paint and sand or airbrush acrylic primers to eliminate the brush texture.

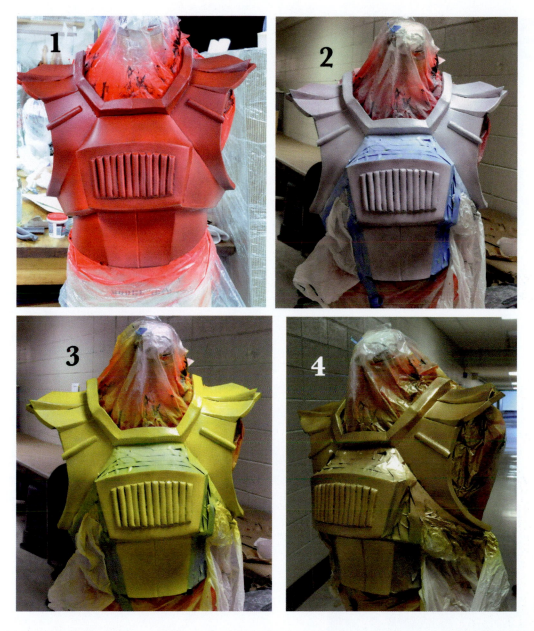

Figure 24-10: The painting process begins by applying several layers of red spray paint, then mask off the selected areas to apply a white undercoat. The yellow layer is added to brighten up the final layer of gold spray paint. *Note*: spray paint and gloss finish can make the foam armor less flexible. Try airbrushing with latex or acrylic paint. Then finish with a clear gloss sealer such as *Modpodge*.

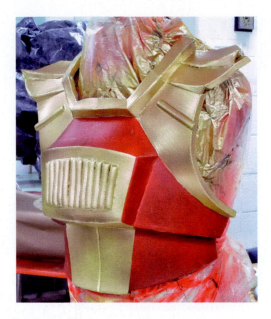

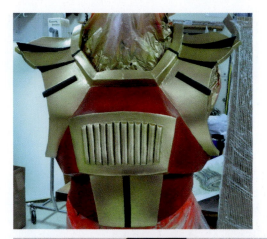

Figure 24-11: Breastplate after masking is removed.

Figure 24-12:
A. Top. Hand-painted details done with latex paint. It is possible to use oil-based or polymer-based paint such as nail polish on areas that will not flex.
B. Bottom. Final painting with airbrush and gloss clear coat finish.

Figure 24-13: Finished armor.

chapter twenty-five

patterned and carved raptor

This project used closed-cell foam (L 200).

Figure 25-1: Start with the design.

Figure 25-2: Working drawings and pared down shape.

Figure 25-3: Building a positive sculpt. Masking tape and paper foundation mounted on a wooden stand.

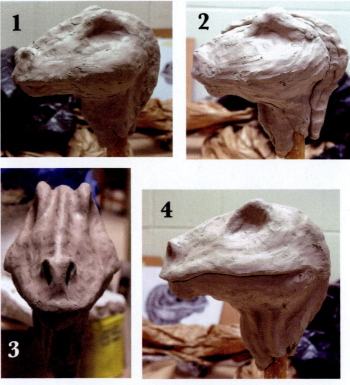

Figure 25-4: Creating the positive sculpt.

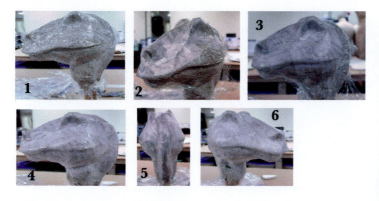

Figure 25-5: To make the pattern skin, use plastic and tape.

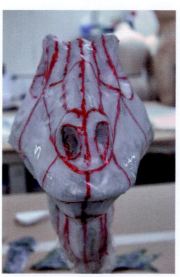
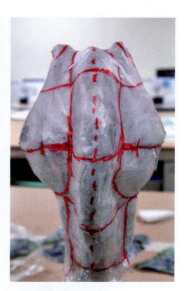

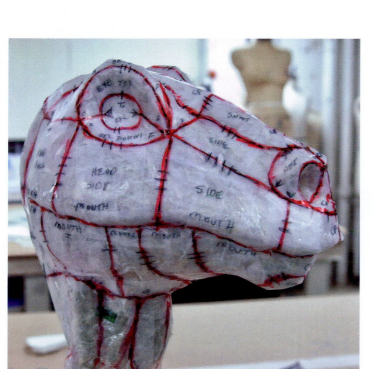

Figure 25-6: Draw the center dividing line then initial pattern lines with red marker.

Figure 25-7: Go over red lines with black marker and add notations.

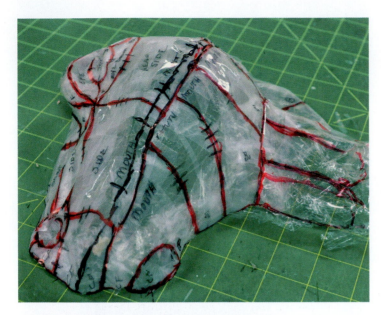

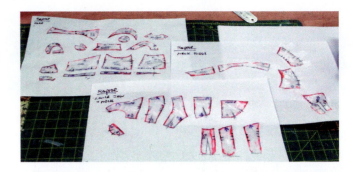

Figure 25-9: All pieces divided and taped to sheet for copying.

Figure 25-10: Pieces are then enlarged roughly 400 percent.

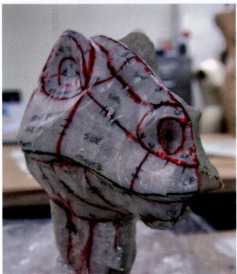

Figure 25-8: Of the two sides of the head, choose the side that is the most visually appealing. Then cut off half of the skin down the center dividing line. The other half of the skin remains on the sculpt for reference.

Figure 25-11: Foam pieces cut out and divided into *right-* and *left-side* piles.

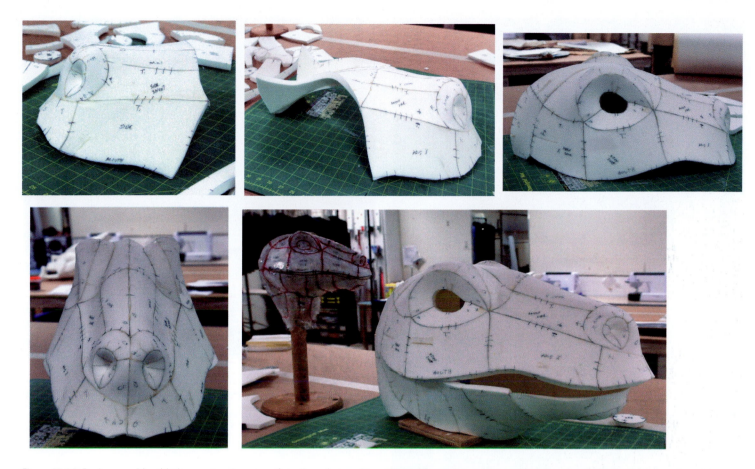

Figure 25-12: Begin assembly with the snout and progress from there. Image shows the positive sculpt and the resulting foam head side by side.

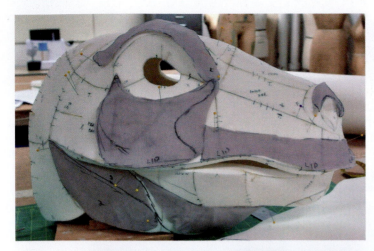

Figure 25-14: Adding in foam mouth plate.

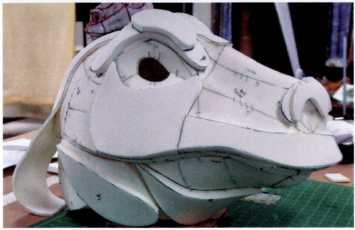

Figure 25-13: Laying on fabric pieces to decide where to add additional thickness for carving.

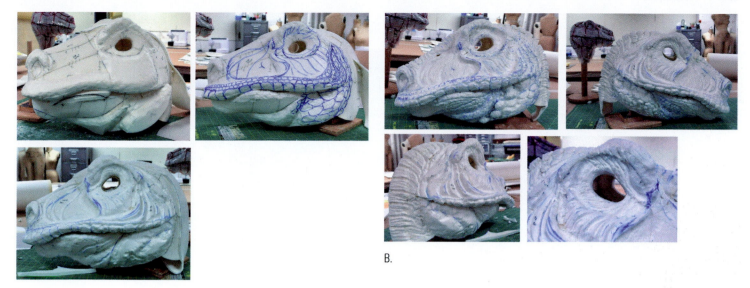

B.

A.

Figure 25-15: Beginning to carve big areas with razor blades.

A. When a large part of the excess foam has been reduced, lines can be added (with chalk or marker) where detail needs to be etched.

B. Carve details with a dremel tool. Different bits will give different effects.

A.

B.

C.

Figure 25-16: The tongue.

A. Cutting 1-inch L 200 on band saw.

B. Sanding down sharp edges and shaping contours.

C. Using a dremel tool to carve center muscle line and pores.

A.   B.

Figure 25-17: Adding the eyes.
A. Left. Using a half of a sanded plastic egg wrapped and glued in place with 1/8-inch fun foam (L 200).
B. Right. Fun foam comes in a variety of colors and textures. The pebbly texture here was perfect. A dremel was used to smooth the added layer into the existing socket.

Figure 24-18: The final unpainted raptor head with neck attached after sanding to refine edges. Before painting, three coats of spray *Plasti Dip* were added to help seal and reinforce the foam.

Figure 25-19: Painting. Head underpainted with browns and laying in rough contour shading. Apply several layers of greens, then add highlights with the dry brush technique.

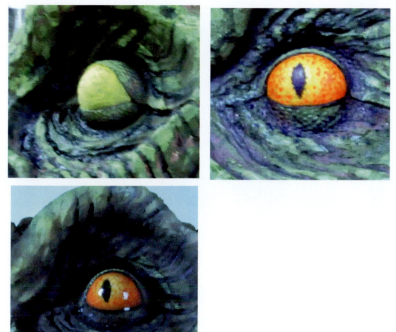

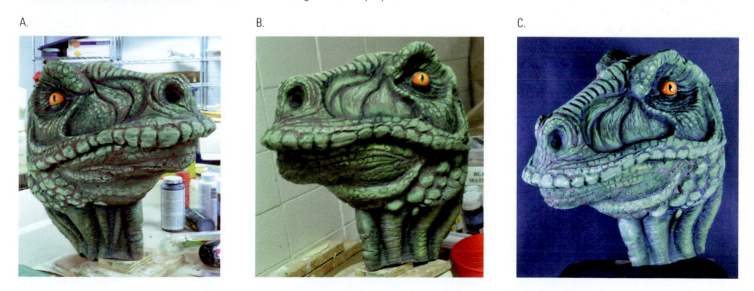

Figure 25-20: The eye is painted lime green. A layer of yellow is applied and detail painted with tiny brushes. The pupil is added last. The final gloss coat is epoxy adhesive.

A.   B.   C.

Figure 25-21A–C: After looking at the painting color and coverage from different angles (and under another light source), I noticed that it needed more refinements.

A.

B.

Figure 25-22A and B: Finished raptor.

appendices

Suppliers and Sources

Tools and General Supplies

Lowes, Harbor Freight, Home Depot
razor blades, adhesives, sandpaper, polystyrene,
L 200 foam anti-fatigue mats

Adhesives

Locktite Company
Simalfa

Faux Fur Sources

Distinctive Fabrics
Fabric.com
Syfabrics.com

Foam Suppliers

Foam Mart

Art supplies

Dick Blick
Texas Art Supply
Cheap Joes Art Supplies

Craft Supplies

Michaels
A E Moore
Hobby Lobby

Latex and Neoprene

Chicago latex
Burman Industries Inc.

Cold Foam

BJB Industries

Pre-fabricatd Rigid Urethane Panels

General Plastics

Unusual Dodads

Thrift stores
Recycling bin

Bibliography

1. American Chemistry Council Website
   "History of Polyurethanes"
   ©2005–2015 American Chemistry Council, Inc. The ACC mark, Responsible Care®, the hands logo mark, CHEMTREC®, TRANSCAER®, and americanchemistry.com are registered service marks of the American Chemistry Council, Inc.
2. Dow Building Solutions Website. Building Dow.com. "The Invention of Styrofoam".
   Copyright © The Dow Chemical Company (1995–2015). All Rights Reserved. ®MT* Trademark of The Dow Chemical Company ("Dow") or an affiliated company of Dow.
3. Wikipedia.org
   "Styrene. Occurrence, History and Use".
   Wikipedia® is a registered trademark of the Wikimedia Foundation, Inc., a non-profit organization. April 8, 2015.

Additional Websites to Aid with Scaling Patterns

1. http://jbwid.com/scalcalc.htm – a scale calculator
2. http://webpages.charter.net/sinkwich/sdventure/html/sd_scalecalc2.htm

3. http://www.wikihow.com/Scale-Drawings-Using-the-Grid-Method
4. http://www.Thesketchbookartistl.com

index

Note: Page numbers followed by "f" refer to figures and followed by "t" refer to tables.